The Intercultural Performance Handbook

What can performers in the West learn from the technical performance traditions of Africa and Asia?

The Intercultural Performance Handbook opens up a new world of technique for performers. The first ever full-length, fully illustrated manual for practitioners, it provides:

- A guide to the physical, vocal and improvisational dynamics drawn from world performance styles
- A new vocabulary with which to interpret plays from around the globe
- Games to use for exploring rhythm, movement, balance, tension and gesture, breathwork, stylisation, and the use of the voice
- A practical, hands-on approach to creating vibrant theatrical work.

Studies on intercultural performance are usually written by scholars and researchers. John Martin explains the definition and development of intercultural performance from the perspective of an experienced practitioner. He provides exercises, practical advice and a clear training process for the inquiring performer or director.

This book is a process of discovery, carefully written so as to develop understanding and move towards empowerment for the adventurous theatre-maker.

John Martin is a theatre director and teacher. He is Director of the Pan Centre for Intercultural Arts, a London-based performance research unit.

The Intercultural Performance Handbook

John Martin

Routledge
Taylor & Francis Group

LONDON AND NEW YORK

First published 2004
by Routledge
11 New Fetter Lane, London EC4P 4EE

Simultaneously published in the USA and Canada
by Routledge
29 West 35th Street, New York, NY 10001

Routledge is an imprint of the Taylor & Francis Group

© 2004 John Martin
Illustrations © 2004 Dwaraki

Typeset in Janson by
HWA Text and Data Management, Tunbridge Wells
Printed and bound in Great Britain by
TJ International Ltd, Padstow, Cornwall

British Library Cataloguing in Publication Data
A catalogue record for this book is available from the British Library

Library of Congress Cataloging in Publication Data
Martin, John, 1951–
    The intercultural performance handbook / John Martin
        p. cm.
1. Movement (Acting) 2. Improvisation (Acting) 3. Voice culture.
I. Title.
    PN2071.M6M37 2003
    792´.028–dc21   2003007184

ISBN 0–415–28187–3 (hbk)
ISBN 0–415–28188–1 (pbk)

To all those from whom I have learned
And to all those who may learn from me

For Shanti

Contents

CONTENTS

Figures

About the author

John Martin is a theatre director, researcher and teacher.

His training and subsequent work in theatre have been in many countries and have absorbed many influences.

He has directed over 50 productions in Britain, France, Sweden, Germany, India and South Africa and his work has toured world-wide.

Parallel to directing he has been consistently engaged in running creative training workshops for actors and students in drama schools in many countries. For ten years he was Artistic Director of the International Theatre Workshop, Scheersberg, Germany; he founded the Commonwealth Theatre Laboratory in Bhopal, India, the Vidya slum actors project in Ahmedabad, and he is the artistic director of the Pan Centre for Intercultural Arts in London, specialising in exploring new possibilities for the arts in multicultural environments. His work has concentrated on developing new standards of richness through intercultural work, whether this is in professional performances or community events.

About the illustrator

Dwaraki created these illustrations during a period as Artist in Residence for the Rangayana Theatre Company in Mysore, India. He is a much respected fine artist who has had numerous exhibitions throughout the country.

Acknowledgements

I gladly acknowledge the many sources from which my working methods have evolved. These include many teachers and colleagues whose work has inspired me. In particular I recognise the great influence of my first 'gurus': Jacques Lecoq, Veronica Sherbourne and Monica Pagneux. I have also gained enormously from the many colleagues at the International Theatre Workshop in Scheersberg, Germany and the master-teachers at Pan's Intercultural Summer Schools in the Performing Arts. Most of all this work is due to the collaboration of the many members of the Pan-Centre for Inter-cultural Arts with whom these ideas, exercises and games have been evolved and tested.

Finally my thanks to the British Council who have supported me during my theatre work throughout the world and made possible the meetings which led to this book.

Author's note

For many years I resisted writing this book. Many actors and workshop participants have asked me for notes on how I have worked with them. They would always ask me why I did not document and publish my 'method'.

The major reason was that although they saw it as a 'method', I did not. It was always changing, growing, questioning itself, developing new ideas. As it was not fixed how could I write it? Or was I afraid that writing it would fix it unalterably?

Well it is still changing and will go on changing, but what I have written is where the work stands now.

I was also aware that committing to print a process which I normally teach by urging participants to experience for themselves would be very difficult. I would have to pre-judge what they were likely to experience; otherwise the next step would not be possible.

This was the most difficult aspect and I hope I have left sufficient space for the all-important personal experience and discovery.

My final fear was that the book would be picked up by someone unfamiliar with my work and that it would be totally misunderstood and misrepresented. So be it. Some of the greatest personal discoveries have resulted from misinterpretations!

So, with all these problems, why did I change my mind?

I am grateful to Ziki Kofoworola of the Centre for Nigerian Cultural Studies at Ahmadu Bello University, Nigeria. After conducting a workshop there he pointed out to me that my hesitation to document my work was denying it to others, and was very selfish.

The realisation that he was right goaded me to undertake the job.

B. V. Karanth's offer to work with his new company-in-training in Mysore, India, gave me the ideal opportunity, and the process of committing these methods to paper began there. It has been revised and added to as a result of many workshops and rehearsal periods inside the Pan Centre for Intercultural Arts and elsewhere.

I offer this manual as a step by step path of creative training for modern performers, to prepare their 'instrument' for theatre work which reflects the new cultural complexity of our exciting, changing world.

I hope all who read it will use it freely as a catalyst for their own creative work.

This intercultural world

AN ONGOING MODEL

The last hundred years have seen our cultural awareness and cultural realities change more radically than ever before. We now live in a world where people of different cultures and ethnicities meet and mix freely, creating a dynamic space for re-assessment of our identities, and opportunities for our performing arts to be enriched and to reflect the societies in which we live.

Not only have travel and transport allowed the more privileged and adventurous to witness and, to some degree, experience many of the world's cultures, they have also brought performance forms from these cultures to wider audiences around the globe. Seeing European theatre in Delhi or Chinese dance in London is no longer a rare treat but part of a regular programme of festivals, tours and cultural exchanges.

Exposure to these forms provides a meeting point of cultures and at meeting points there is always some sort of exchange. In the performing arts such meetings have a history of being enormously enriching. At the individual level an artist sees something inspiring in another way of working and something of that experience is transferred into his or her work. This new work, this new hybrid, is the starting point of interculturalism.

At the broader level of groups, clans, tribes or nations such inter-actions have permeated the history of peoples as they have met, whether in peace or in oppression, and have forged endless new forms of expression. This phenomenon has accelerated enormously in the last century with mass migrations of peoples on an unprece-dented scale.

This exchange is not multiculturalism, the simultaneous existence of several cultures side by side, nor cross-culturalism where people from one cultural background learn a form from another culture and practise it. Interculturalism is an area of interaction where new forms are created.

Interculturalism is of course not only a 'western' phenomenon. The great theatrical forms of Japan are the result of dramatic dances and rituals which moved eastwards from Korea meeting the culture of the native Japanese. The music of north India is the result of the influence of Persian instrumentation brought with the Muslim rulers, and many of the stories of the Chinese 'operas' are derived from Buddhism as it spread from India. Contemporary European and American dance and music have many of their roots deep in African culture and the African diaspora, and Indonesian performance styles have absorbed stories and styles from incoming Indian Hinduism and the later spread of Islam.

EUROPEAN MODERN THEATRE – THE OTHER SOURCES

In European theatre the inspiration from non-European performance styles is so substantial that it can certainly be argued that the cutting edge of twentieth and twenty-first century theatre would not have existed without it. So many of the seminal theatre-makers of the last century were deeply influenced by theatre from beyond their immediate cultures that contemporary European theatre is deeply touched by a strand of interculturalism.

From Artaud's revelations on seeing Balinese theatre, through Copeau's work with Japanese performers in the Vieux Colombier company, and Brecht's deep and lasting impressions on seeing Mei Lan Fang of the Beijing Opera, we have a history of influences which have revolutionised European theatre.

Grotowski searched for greater understanding of the actor's art by studying exercises from Kathakali and beyond, Peter Brook tried to uncover a force beyond the culturally specific in his multicultural companies and Eugenio Barba began to analyse dynamics in world theatre which, through understanding, can enrich us. Robert Lepage has drawn from Bunraku, Berkoff from Kabuki, and Ariane Mnouchkine from styles, pictures, rhythms and colours of many

Asian theatrical forms to shape her stunning contemporary theatre. The list is long. All have found something which enriched their work and lifted it from the constraints of European psychological realism. That 'something' may have been different in each case, but this list of people, and there are many more, shows how deeply contemporary Western theatre has been influenced by intercultural factors.

This modernisation of theatre through interaction with other cultures exists across the world. Badal Sircar's Satabdi company in Kalkata benefited from improvisation techniques from European and American theatre teachers, while Nobel laureate Wole Soyinka adapted European play-structures to explore very African issues, and fellow Nigerian, Ola Rotimi, adapted classical Greek themes to reflect on local tradition and psychology.

In short the ability of artists to be excited by other ways of presenting material is endless and their ability to allow their work to reflect this excitement is the essence of their creativity. It has existed throughout history as an inevitable product of the meetings of peoples, and has led to many of the cultural forms we now perceive as classical. It is at least as strong as its direct antithesis – the desire and attempt to keep a cultural form 'pure' by passing down every detail unchanged from generation to generation. Of course both tendencies are possible within a society, one preserving the past, the other reflecting the developments within communities.

The twenty-first century finds us in an even more interactive cultural position. Mass migrations of people as a result of colonisation, political oppression, natural disaster, labour or economic needs have created a cultural mix of vast proportions in countless population centres. Major cities on all continents have populations of a wide ethnic, and therefore cultural, span. London alone has more than 300 language groups, New Delhi has inhabitants from the Dravidian south, Aryan north, tribal centre and Sino-Tibetan northeast, Beijing draws from all modern China's ethnic groups, while Melbourne, Toronto and New York all claim to be the most multicultural city in the world.

The meetings of ethnicities and cultures are no longer at the end of a long journey, they are just across the street, and this juxtaposition has enormous consequences for our ways of expressing our hopes and fears, our stories and needs through performance. Where some people may see these migrations as a political and social problem, the artist is able to see them as an enrichment.

For while those leaders of modern theatre sought inspiration from other cultures to redefine and enrich their theatre in the face of the perceived paucity of naturalism, current intercultural performance is a reflection of the realities of our populations. It is, therefore, at once enriching stylistically and resonant socially.

This is exactly where the challenge lies for the contemporary theatre-maker. We cannot deny that the majority of European theatre is stuck in an historical cul-de-sac, exploring themes of Caucasian peoples, using naturalistic or realistic styles and performing to largely Caucasian audiences. Outside, in the streets, in the schools, in the shops, races and cultures mix and interact. Inside the theatres we do not reflect this and, with some notable exceptions, we remain conservatively in denial of it.

Contrast this with music, the most promiscuous of the performing arts, where cross-cultural meetings regularly throw up new and exciting hybrids, which become new forms, popular or esoteric, which go on, in their turn, to further hybridise.

Contrast it with our eating habits where new tastes merge, new ingredients become available and a hundred hybrid cuisines are created, not just commercially but in the normal kitchens of normal people.

The challenge in theatre is to create new work which resonates with its populations so that as society changes theatre can reflect its hopes and fears in a style which is rich and accessible.

Intercultural performance, therefore, is not one style, not one thing; it is an ongoing process of meeting, cross-pollinating and producing new and relevant work for its surroundings. As long as peoples and cultures meet there will be new ideas, new ways of communicating and creating.

Intercultural theatre does not challenge the existence of traditional styles. Many are of great beauty wherever they are performed. Interculturalism provides a forum where their practitioners can meet, find commonalities and move on to create new work which is as resonant as those traditional styles were when they were first created.

It is very common for a newly arrived ethnic group to want to hold on to its cultural form as a reminder of its place of origin and lifestyle and to maintain its identity in an alien country. Such continuation, however, often leads to such forms being frozen in time and resisting change much more than in the country of origin.

However, in the second and third generations it is equally common for these groups to interact freely with the host culture or cultures in order to communicate and share. This is where the meetings and new forms may occur. The result and reflection of those meetings are our starting point.

This process of interculturalism is vast and we must, as performers from all backgrounds, look to how we can enrich and inform our work in the midst of this changing cultural world. Whether it is a European performer re-discovering, through exposure to other traditions, the heightened celebratory theatrical worlds which were lost in the Industrial Revolution, or an Asian performer looking at the psychological realism of Western theatre to enrich work in theatre for social change, or an African performer paralleling story-telling forms from his/her culture with those of India or the Caribbean, we have a multiplicity of routes.

In my own work I have looked for commonalities between cultures, meeting points, sparking points, complementary approaches rather than contrasts. I have sought dynamics we can share, or re-discover, to make new forms. Interculturalism is not a juxtaposition of styles, it is a new result from a new meeting.

So the meeting of Indian, European and Nigerian cultures in *Itan Kahani–The Story of Stories* produced a modern style of story-telling theatre which was hugely popular in the UK, India and West Africa. The production of *Guardians of The Deep*, created for Theatre for Africa and the Johannesburg Earth Summit, had actor-musicians from seven nationalities whose skills could interact to create a performance reflecting the conditions of local fishermen throughout the world in the face of globalisation. Their common skills showed a community which could be recognised by audiences internationally.

In India the Vidya project uses elements drawn from Gujarati Bhavai, elements of folk music, of Bollywood songs, of South American Forum Theatre and many of the principles in this book, to make an interactive hybrid style targeted at discussing issues around girl-children in the slums of Ahmedabad.

When we started the Pan Centre for Intercultural Arts we knew the task of facilitating intercultural performance would be enormous. It was to provide a forum for the many theatrical traditions in the UK and other countries where it has subsequently worked.

Very quickly we realised that to benefit from the many background traditions within our society the available actor training techniques were inadequate. This was equally true for a Chinese performer wishing to understand Yoruba culture as for a British performer looking at Kathakali. In the midst of many hundreds of cultures it is not possible, nor ultimately desirable, to spend many years studying each one. So we sought some practical methods to enlarge our cultural vocabulary as a preparation for stage work.

These methods are distilled from many thousands of hours spent with traditional teachers of performance styles from across the world, and many years of practical work by the performers of Pan, people from many different cultural and stylistic backgrounds, in rehearsal, in performance and in running workshops across the world. It is also the result of collaborations with performance companies in workshops and festivals and many meetings with remarkable artists living in our modern cities but forging their own new styles of speaking to their audiences.

With every meeting the methods evolve, but those which are included in this book are a bedrock for performers who want to increase their creative work, their physical and vocal range. These methods will certainly improve their ability to work in naturalistic and realistic works, but are equally valuable in interpreting plays written for a more heightened style like those of Girish Karnad or Wole Soyinka (or William Shakespeare or Euripides!). Mostly they will allow performers to enter into a new world of theatre vocabulary where they can create their own work in a style which is valuable, entertaining and accessible for their own audience in their own situation.

PRACTICAL STEPS TO INTERCULTURAL PERFORMANCE

The path of discovery of an actor is to find a level of honesty, of truth in yourself and in your work, so that your audience opens to you and does not, subconsciously, feel tricked. With this honesty you will never feel you are fooling your audience, never feel distanced from it, sceptical, cold, even disinterested.

But what can we use to clearly express such truth?

Our goal must be clarity and precision – finding the exact use of our bodies, our timing, our voices, so that we communicate exactly what we want to say.

This is why we train, to prepare the instrument to be played. Training is not an end in itself, nor is it to be able to display great virtuosity, but it is to be able to communicate clearly the right message at the right moment.

A prerequisite for this communication is that the actor must have '*presence*' – that quality which, like a magnet, draws the audience's attention to him or her.

This is not a mystical quality which some have and some do not. There are elements in this presence which we can learn and absorb, and, having learned it, this presence is in the actor, not just in the character. Before the actor takes on the character it is there … it is *pre-expressive*. This is a term used as an observation by theatre analysts, particularly Eugenio Barba in his work at the International School of Theatre Anthropology (ISTA), but here we shall look at practical ways of reaching and using this state.

What gives us this presence? The word '*energy*' is our key. Presence is the correct control of our energy.

For our purpose we must take energy as it is perceived by performers and audience. Of course there are scientific definitions which we should not ignore but we are talking of theatre-energy.

When an actor is in control of his or her energy it not only makes the performance more dynamic for us but it is as if the audience can also feel this 'charge', this 'electricity' which fills the stage and reaches out to them.

In the Japanese theatre the concept of 'ki', in Chinese theatre the 'chi' are energies taught as being latent in the body – ready to be awakened and channelled. The 'kundalini' of yoga, the grounded position and contact with the earth of Nigerian dance, all speak of this energy as a very tangible entity – and every performer who works to discover and experience it will also feel the energy as a very definite force. (Of course in scientific systems like acupuncture this concept of energy generation and flow is well understood.)

In our practical experience, as well as in the theories of many theatre forms, martial arts and meditative techniques, we find that energy has a given source-area in the body. Invariably this is centred in that band which encircles the body from the abdomen to the base of the spine. In the front and centre of the body it is where the pressure commences for activating the breathing; in the back it is where the spine emerges from the pelvis, the focal and distribution point of the central spinal nerve.

The images for this centre and the energy emanating from it are numerous – a fire which spreads heat throughout the body, a snake which mounts the spine, even a heavy iron ball suspended in the pelvis, wrapped in soft cotton, giving momentum and weight.

Through rooting the breathing deeply and through awakening the muscles and nerves of this area, the centre can soon be felt. Some Chinese actors wear a tight belt around this area (below the normal waist level) and I have found that wearing tight elastic around this band works as reminder of where this zone is.

Becoming aware of this centre we must use it to change our action. Offstage we tend to walk stiffly, our legs locking straight at the knees. As soon as we 'unlock' our knees and keep them slightly bent, the centre is lower and 'sprung' and the action can flow from it. It can lead us, stop us, be the source for any direction and any action.

It is this position, or some variant of it, which we see in most sub-Saharan African dance-drama, in the Noh Theatre basic position, in Kathakali, in the low-flowing walk of the Beijing Opera, and in the many martial arts forms where bright alertness and readiness are all-important. Just putting our body in this position we feel more alert, more aware – as if a mist lifts from our senses.

Onto this base we build the breathing, the active way of charging our bodies, quite literally, giving the body the oxygen it needs, but also developing that flow of inward and outward energy which gives our every movement its life and its rhythm.

It still astonishes me how little attention is given to breathing and all its active and expressive possibilities. It is normally only taught as a base for song or voice work (where it is, of course, vital), but this is only part of its importance.

It was the great teacher Jacques Lecoq in Paris who inspired my thinking about the links between breathing and action, and the ideas in this book have grown from those gratefully received seeds.

The *centre* and the *breathing* are the bases of the strong, flexible and active body we need for *presence*. Many more factors complete the dynamic presence we need (we shall particularly deal with the eyes), but there is one other pre-expressive state which is vital to the creative actor.

It is *'playfulness'*.

Many artists tend to shy away from this word as too childish or demeaning. However, that free flow of ideas which we experience as children, and that total absorption and seamless, ever-changing game we see in the play of young animals, are qualities indispensable to a creative artist. And the joy of playing should underpin all our work. When children play, even at being aggressive, we still feel the joy of their playing behind it.

If the actor's work always contains this 'pre-expressive playfulness' the audience will also enjoy and be part of the creativity; they will feel involved in it and be open to what you are communicating.

Playfulness is particularly vital for actors who face the challenge of creating new work, writing, devising, even setting up their own groups. They must have that ability to allow inspiration and ideas to freely flow in practice, not just in the mind but out on the rehearsal floor.

Playfulness is also a state which makes our training richer. Exercises cease to be 'only exercises', and become material to be played with, examined for associations, feelings and possibilities. After the technical learning and mastery of any exercise this helps us bring it to life.

It always seems wrong to me, as happens in so many training programmes and drama schools, that there are technique exercises (normally split into movement and voice), there are improvisation classes, scene classes and then there are rehearsals. And no bridges between them. No way for the actor to know how to use one for the other! It is as if training physically and vocally were enough, and that somehow, magically, the complete osmosis will take place in rehearsal and on stage. Quite the opposite is true. Although exercises taught this way are not useless, they are limited. They make you flexible and fit. They give you 'skills' which can be manipulated by directors. But often I see actors or student actors who are physically flexible and dynamic in a movement class, or who have developed a three-octave vocal range in the voice class, and yet when they come on stage their bodies are stiff and their voices are strangulated.

Why? Because their own inner blocks and protective barriers take them back to 'safe' zones, and because the exercises have never been developed to take them into 'playing', and 'playing' has never been introduced as an essential ingredient of acting.

The first chapter of this book concentrates on awakening the energy and putting it into play. With this complete you will be taken through exercises in the second chapter which show how different applications of that energy lead you to different types of mood, emotion, characterisation and situation.

These are based on a psycho-physical realisation that different moods and situations cause different energy states. By starting with an understanding of these energy states we can rediscover the emotional states.

It is the antithesis of the 'method' training in which an internal psychological artifice is constructed to give truth to the character. The danger with the method approach is that the emotions may be completely felt by the actor, but never visible for an audience. The methods in this book start with the visible, the positions, states and contradictions of the body, and root them back to the feelings. Thus the visible communication factor, so necessary in theatre, is always present.

This is a path used in many theatre forms around the world. Perhaps the clearest example is in the south Indian theatre form, Kathakali, where young students learn the complex facial expressions which represent the nine basic emotional states. When they first learn them it looks like nothing more than impressive control of face muscles which most of us never isolate; impressive but empty.

It is a few years later, as the students mature, and learn to 'fill' these learned face masks with their own experiences and understanding of the characters, that these impressive expressions become moving, complex and, of course, highly visible.

It would be wrong to see this approach as in conflict with psychologically developed character development. Both are searching for a credible character and a way of communicating it. They are both part of a continuum, but this book works from physical energies as a starting point.

In the third chapter the book takes you into an area of work which is intrinsic to so many forms of theatre but which is rarely taught as a means of exploration and almost never in schools of realistic theatre. It is the use of *rhythm*. I know that many performers assert, or fear, that they have no sense of rhythm, but Bisi Adigun's observation holds that 'if you can walk you have rhythm' and these exercises are to take you easily into a body awareness of rhythm.

You will discover how using rhythm delivers sharp clarity to movement, gesture and words, opens up new possibilities for characterisation and takes us right into that area we normally call 'timing'.

In the fourth chapter you will look at *improvisation*, an area of our theatre work which is not normally associated with non-European forms of performance. In fact improvisation, in a variety of ways, is extremely present across the world from African dance theatre to Japanese and Balinese drama.

These exercises draw on many sources to use the feeling of playfulness to circumvent the internal 'censor' voice which so often blocks the route to our creativity. By following them you will develop an ease of improvisation which will allow a freshness and ability to reinvent constantly in devising, in rehearsal and in performance. Before any exercises, especially if you are not particularly fit, stretch the body gently, or jog to warm the body and increase blood flow.

The final chapter looks at the *voice* as another use of the body's energy, introducing ways of unblocking and controlling that energy. This is an excellent way to discover a voice which can be used with strong physical action and the exercises draw from many techniques of outdoor vocal work such as working songs, and include a special adaptation of an Indian exercise normally done standing in a fast flowing river!

Thus the book carries you through the most essential uses of your energy as an actor, how they are linked to your feelings and how they can transform your body for a new situation or new character. Finally, of course, it is for you to customise what works for you and develop it. That is in the tradition of creativity. It is how ideas came to me and how I can pass them on.

1 Discovering the energy

This chapter introduces you to the process of finding the energy we all possess within us, and shows you how to draw from that the alertness we need in any type of performance.

What do we mean by energy? It is something very practical and very useable. It is felt by the performer and by the audience.

When we see actors from Kathakali, Noh Theatre or the Beijing Opera we sense that they have an inner energy supporting the role they are playing. We often sense that this energy is much greater than that which is being used in performance, but which has huge latent potential. In Noh there is a tenet: Feel in the heart ten, but show in the body only seven. It implies that the audience should always feel that much more is possible at any moment, giving a sense of potentiality, almost of danger.

This energy is not only seen in high action. It can also be like that of a cat poised to pounce, totally still but an obvious energy held in every part of the body. This is a wonderful starting image for an actor. Even in stillness there is enormous held energy.

We also see it in a number of martial arts. The energy is ready for anything, centred, alert and constantly on 'the edge of danger' as performer-trainer Olu Taiwo calls it.

This alertness opens us to the feelings we need as actors and prepares us for the vital transmission of those feelings to an audience. Audiences respond readily to energy on stage. We often call it 'presence', but presence is only how we awaken and hold our energy.

The exercises to introduce these concepts to you cover:

- Body shape, vertical line and centre
- Stability
- Breathing – on the second element of energy
- Breathing – centred for energy – jumps
- Resistance
- States and energies within the breathing
- Energy and eyes
- Energy in kneeling and sitting.

BODY SHAPE, VERTICAL LINE AND CENTRE

Exercise 1 The empty pot

Preparing for the work of performance.

This is adapted from an exercise taught by a Kabuki actor. It helps you to be aware of the shape of your body in space, and see it as a receptacle for the characters and creative ideas which will fill it. It is an excellent exercise to start the day.

Stand with your feet slightly apart, arms relaxed, eyes closed. Feel as if you are emptying yourself. Release any tensions, empty any thought or cares from the outside world. Be like an empty pot.

Then, feeling the feet firmly on the floor, be aware of the shape of the body (the pot) into which impulses will flow, through which expressions will flow. Feel the outside surface of your body. Mentally trace it from the soles of your feet up the front of your body, over your head and down the back of your body to the ankles. This is the shape you make in space.

Breathe freely into this empty space, as if the breath were flowing into every part of it from the tips of the toes to the top of the skull. As you breathe deeper you will feel a slight inner pressure of air inside this prepared body. The breath is giving you the first feeling of your latent energy. It is filling you.

1 In a commentary on the Indian Natya Shastra the actor's body is described as a wine glass (or cup). Its job is to receive the wine (the play) and to pass it to the lips of the drinker (the audience). The role is thus to be a 'good wine glass', empty of other elements and pleasing to look at. Any dirt or deformity would spoil the appreciation of the wine.

Without losing this feeling open the eyes – take in the impulses around you. See them as new, as if for the first time.[1]

Exercise 2 The rope

Adapted from a Native American director's exercise shared at The Commonwealth Theatre Laboratory, Bhopal.

Feel the feet firmly on the floor. Feel the spine growing upwards as if it is part of a rope stretching from the centre of the earth up to the sky. You are on this line wherever you go. Feel the pull up through the spine to the sky, and from the base of the spine down through the legs into the earth. They are opposing pulls along the vertical. Feel the energy of this opposition and the energy up and down this vertical column.

This is a very basic awareness of the extra energy 'born' of a simple counter-tension, in this case between up and down.

Exercise 3 Running on the rope

Start a gentle run on one spot, still feeling the same verticality, the heels touching the ground on each step and the spine still stretching upwards (on that rope). The shoulders, ribs and pelvis are not tense, nor over-relaxed, but suspended from the vertical. Avoid any side-ways wobbling. The feeling is of energy being gathered on each downbeat of the heels as if the ground is a 'battery' from which to draw power – rising up each leg to meet at the base of the spine – rising up the spine to leave through the eyes, as if the eyes are an extension of the spine.

Exercise 4 Centring

Continue the run as above. Vigorously massage the abdominal area from just above the navel down to the top of the pubic bone and round to the base of the spine, as if you were wearing a belt of energy. You will feel the blood flowing there. Keeping that awareness drop from the run into a low centred position (see Figure 1.1), knees bent (knees vertically above the feet), legs open and spine still vertical. The eyes are alert, the arms open and the legs are like a sprung spring. The energy is centred in the abdomen and base of the spine where you massaged. From the run this drop should be very strong but very light, the landing should be like a cat's – virtually soundless and ready for any subsequent action. If you drop too heavily, and thus noisily, the downward energy prevents a state of readiness.

Practise constant changing between the vertical running and the centred position. On landing in this very important position there is a sense of anticipation, of readiness (it is very still and very charged) as this is a position from which action can begin. You are experiencing the powered position which has drawn theatre-makers to realise the energy of stillness inherent in so many styles of theatre from Topeng to Kathakali, and common in many martial arts forms.

From such a position you can run, jump, fall or twist in an instant.[2]

Extensions

1   Move around the space in a gentle run. On a given signal drop into this centred position.

2   Move around the space, running. Drop into the centred position in your own timing, whenever you feel an impulse. For example you may hear something, become aware of a change in light, meet someone's eyes; all these are impulses to drop into the centred position. You may end up facing someone or something. What is your relationship to it?

2 Beijing Opera teacher, Ma Ming Qun, wore a cord around his abdomen, which he tightened exactly on the point where he feels the chi, to give him a tangible reminder of this energy.

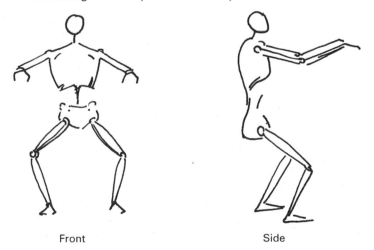

Front   Side

Figure 1.1 The centered position

3   Note then how you leave this position to continue running. You have to leave the state of heightened tension very carefully, not just walk out of it.

4   Repeat 2 but walking sometimes fast, sometimes slow, ready for the impulse to 'centre'.

Feel that you carry this centred position in you wherever you go, ready for use.

STABILITY

The strength of the centred position should not be stiff or rigid. Indeed it is not really strong and certainly not stable if it is rigid. The strength should be as of rubber, not of glass. Glass is strong but, as it cannot bend, it will smash. Rubber will give and spring back if pushed.

Therefore if an impulse (a firm push) is given to any part of the body you should be able to accept it, go with it, and return to the centred position, like rubber. This needs a great mobility of the centre. Effectively whatever part of the body is pushed it is counter-balanced either by the pelvis or torso moving either side of a centre-of-gravity line and then returning. If the body reacts strongly and fluidly then the feet do not move and you maintain a strong, workable, stable position, and you feel that you are always in control of your energy.

Pushes to the abdomen, chest, shoulders, under the chin or to the sides of the head and pulls to the arms or from behind the head and shoulders are all possible (see Figure 1.2).

Exercise 5 Stability game

Bringing the energy into play.

Two people stand facing each other in the deep centred position. Establish eye contact. One partner gives an impulse-push on any part of the body to the other who goes with the impulse, then regains stability and in turn gives the next impulse. Continue alternating until each is easily keeping stability. If you find your partner has a particular weakness, concentrate just on that spot.

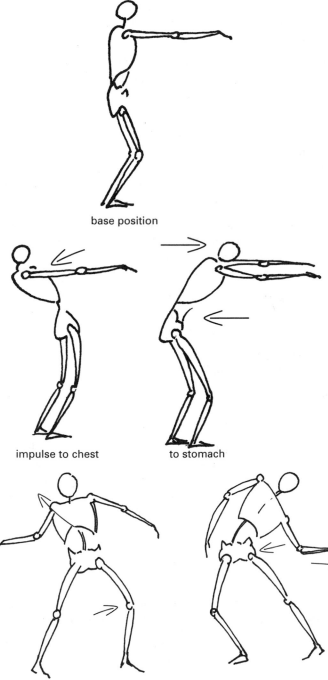

base position

impulse to chest   to stomach

to shoulder or behind knee   to arm or to hip

Figure 1.2 Stability

Start with impulses to the abdomen, the chest, the shoulders, the sides and back of the head. Later a pull on a hand or a push from behind a knee can be tried.

When the abdomen is pushed people tend to try and resist to protect this soft area. In fact it is more protective to yield and go with the received push.

Indeed most people begin by trying to push against the impulse, which creates merely a confrontation of forces where the greater force wins. By accepting the impulse, going with it and regaining balance, you will see how much stronger this is. If you have ever watched the martial arts movement aikido, you will have seen how effective, and beautiful, this is.

Keep the breathing free on being pushed. If you block the breathing there will be unwanted tension in the neck. If you actively exhale while being pushed your movement and recovery become easier and much more fluid.

As you come back to the centre, re-establish eye contact with your partner and inhale. This increases concentration and makes the exercise much more playable.

Keep changing partners. Each one will have different levels of fluidity, resistance and recovery.

Extensions

Ways of regaining position:

1   GEOMETRIC: When the impulse is taken, the body follows it straight to its furthest point, stops, re-starts and goes back to its original position. In other words it follows a straight line, the energy stops, re-starts and retraces the straight line forward.

2   ORGANIC: the impulse is taken but the line of the pushed body part finds a curved line back to its starting point. There is no stop – it is one flowing line.[3]

Developing the game

1   The partners change from 'geometric' to 'organic' at a signal. Notice the differences in the relationship between you.

2   One reacts only with 'geometric', the other 'organic', then change. Notice the difference.

3 We are examining here 'ways of using energy'. Neither is right nor wrong – they are different. They also call up different feelings in the body depending on which one is used (see Chapter 2 Geometric and Organic).

3　Use both types of reaction, changing at will to 'play' with your partner. Also play with changing the speed of your reaction, and the waiting time before giving the next impulse. These are all variables which can express a great deal. Play with them. Soon you have developed beyond a mere exercise into an exchange of action and reaction which starts to read as a human situation, the beginnings of drama.

4　When all the above ideas are flowing freely try exactly the same game but with one metre's space between partners – pushing the impulse across the space. React as if pushed on the point your partner is pushing towards. Then increase the space to 2 metres, then 3, 4, 5 metres so it can be played across a large space. It needs great concentrated precision as well as physical mobility and is an excellent exercise for projecting and communicating across space.

We are still establishing the basic techniques of energy but already the possibility of 'play' has come into them so that they are not just exercises to be repeated, but situations to be explored. This will involve your creativity. Feel free to apply new layers or new situations to these concepts. For example the last exercise could easily take a verbal line: as you project your 'push' across the space send a word with it. Feel the difference in the types of words you send with different pushes. Then take away the physical action of pushing and send only the word, but the other reacts with the body as if pushed off centre by the words themselves. Being pushed off centre (de-stabilised) links you immediately to a psychologically unbalanced state.

BREATHING – THE SECOND ELEMENT OF ENERGY

It seems so simple to state that the breath is our most immediate access to energy. We all know that the oxygen so vital for energy creation enters our body with the breath. Yet most of our concentration on breathing techniques is directed only towards voice production, not towards the powering of our physical vocabulary, and increasing the presence of our movement. Of course in the practice of yoga, in T'ai chi and other martial arts forms these relationships are well established, as they are in some of Lecoq's exercises (e.g. Le Mur). Learning from these we can find much greater control over our awareness and use of energy on stage.

These explorations will link the breath directly to the movement, enabling you to feel the power of different breathing on your psycho-physical state.

Exercise 6 The importance of abdominal breathing

Standing in the deep centred position, place both hands on the abdomen, apply pressure inwards and, by so doing, push the air up and out of the body through an open mouth (avoid vocalising the outward breath).[4]

Hold this position without breathing for as long as is comfortable. Then simply allow the air to rush in. This will happen without conscious muscular effort, as an involuntary action (see Figure 1.3).

Repeat this until the abdomen can be felt to react strongly and until the flow of air from the mouth to the abdomen is direct, without any tension in the neck and particularly without trying to breathe in the upper chest. This upper-chest breathing is seen by a raising and lowering of the collarbone and upper ribs. Breathing so high in

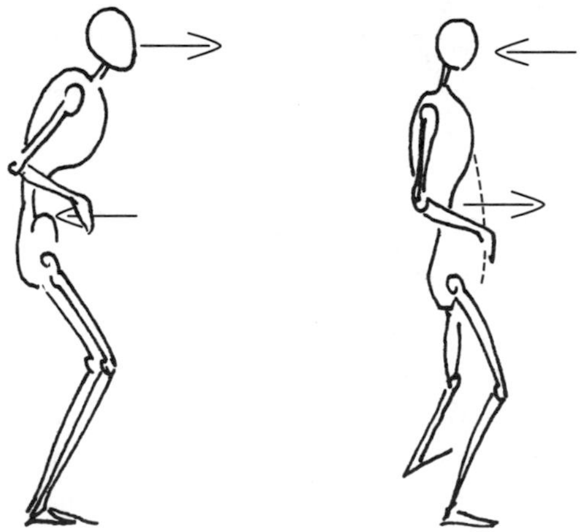

4 You can push quite firmly inwards and then upwards. You are really pushing against the intestines to displace the diaphragm upwards which deflates the lungs and pushes out the air.

push abdomen   air rushes in to
to expel air   push abdomen out

Figure 1.3 Abdominal breathing

the chest not only adds a lot of tension to the upper body and neck (which will cause problems with the voice) but also draws a relatively limited amount of air into the lungs.

Like pouring water into a jug feel the air reach the bottom first and then start filling the space.[5]

RIB BREATHING

When the deep abdominal breathing is established we can then add the other major mechanism to maximise the volume of breath. The expansion of the rib cage naturally increases the volume of the lungs, thus decreasing the air pressure within and causing air to rush in.

The whole rib cage can swing outwards to increase this volume but often it is quite limited. To maximise this effect we can concentrate on the lowest ribs. If these can swing outwards the greatest volume of breath can be achieved.

Place the backs of your hands on the lowest ribs on the sides of your body. Apply moderate pressure to be aware exactly where you have to move the ribs. As you breathe in push against your hands to swing the ribs outwards and slightly upwards like the sides of a bellows. The more movement you achieve there the greater the capacity for air to enter the lungs.

If this is difficult you can work with a partner. Stand behind your partner and place your hands firmly on their lowest ribs. Push gently inwards to give your partner the point to push against. As they breathe in they will attempt to push your hands outwards. As they exhale your pressure will help to push the air out.

Exercise 7 Filling the jug

With one hand on the abdominal muscles and one on the lower ribs try to link the two breathing states we have just explored. Like water pouring into a jug, breathe first into the lowest part of your body by expanding the abdomen and allowing the diaphragm to descend. As this breath completes allow the ribs to swing outwards against your hand and fill the mid-range of your thorax. Breathe out from both areas at the same time. Practise this until the two

5 Although the feeling is that the air flows right down into the stomach and down to the anus and pubic bone (and this is a good image to maintain as a help), in fact what we are pushing is the intestine, the gut. In pushing this inwards it is displaced upwards and thus pushes the diaphragm upwards which pushes the air out. On breathing in the reverse occurs: as the diaphragm descends the intestines are pushed down and displaced forwards. So the area we are manipulating is the 'pump' mechanism for the air, not the area the air reaches.

breathings flow one into the other. Soon you will have maximal capacity which is ready to be used in action.

Exercise 8 Breathing (1)

To feel the inward and outward flow of breath and to link it to the preparation and execution of energy – and to feel the breathing as physical action.

Stand in the centred position with the arms extended horizontally:

1   On the inward breath feel the energy flowing into the centre and draw the hands and arms in towards the body, hands and fingers flexed back (see Figure 1.4).

On the outward breath feel the energy flowing out from the centre along the arms (stretch them), through the fingers (stretch them), and imagine the energy flowing out through the fingers to the walls.

2   As above with the arms and hands but on the inward breath also draw the heels up and feel the energy pulling up towards the centre.

On the outward breath let the energy flow down and push the heels firmly into the floor.[6]

6 The head should stay on one level throughout, so ensure it is not rising and falling with the movement. This means that the centre is still and the focus of the inward and outward tide of your energy.

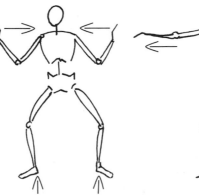 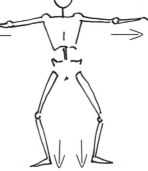

breath and body drawn in   breath and body flowing out

Figure 1.4 Breathing (1)

3   As above with the arms and heels but on the inward breath also narrow the eyes to almost closed as if drawing them inwards.

On the outward breath let the energy flow to and through the eyes. Stretch them wide and imagine a beam of energy flowing from the eyes to the opposite wall.

With all three stages in action repeat it several times. Feel both the inwards and outwards flow of energy and breath and particularly feel the 'held' moment between inwards and outwards breath when there is a strong sense of latent action, with the energy gathered in your centre.

Exercise 9 Breathing (2)

Drawing like a bow, cutting like a knife.

Take a deep centred position, turn the body to face left, both arms stretching out to the left, the shoulders dropped, the right leg stretched.

The inward breath

Leave the left hand in position, pull the right hand across the body as if drawing a bow and continue it through until fully stretched to the right (see Figure 1.5). The weight is transferred to the right side, left leg stretched, and your head is turned to follow the right hand.

starting position   inward breath   end of in-breath
(arrow marks
out-breath)

Figure 1.5 Breathing (2)

23

The outward breath

Describe a semi-circle with the right hand and arm back to the starting position, cutting through the air and transferring the weight back to the left leg. The eyes follow the hand throughout.

Repeat this action 20 to 30 times until the flow in and out enters the movement. Naturally the drawing action of the in-breath will be somewhat faster than the out-breath action which can trace the return with some resistance through the air. Again note and mark the energised moment between in and out breaths. Stillness as strength.

Ensure that the shoulders remain relaxed throughout. The energy flows through them and is not blocked there.

Exercise 10 Breathing (3)

Breath giving strength to action – throwing and hitting.

This is a very easy and very clear way of seeing the astonishing extra strength and meaning which breath lends to an action.

Throwing (or breathing a throw)

Stand with the feet slightly apart. Swing the right arm from behind you, through and up in front of you as if throwing a ball high and forward. All this with no particular breathing.

Now add the breathing – a deep inward breath on the backswing and an outward breath on the upswing (the throw). Feel how the breath aids the action (in-breath for preparation, out-breath for execution). By breathing deeper the 'throw' becomes even stronger.

Try with the left hand. For those who are right-handed the co-ordination will be markedly more difficult. Note how the breathing helps this.

Punching (or breathing a punch)

Stand with your feet comfortably apart. Make a fist with the right hand, pull the elbow back and then punch forward as if hitting something (or someone) about 40 centimetres in front of you. No particular breathing.

Again add the breathing – inward on the pull back, outward on the punch. Make sure the outward breath begins and ends with the beginning and end of the punch.

Notice how you suddenly find power in the punch through application of the breath. This is even more marked when you try punching with your left hand (or right if you are left-handed), which normally feels relatively unco-ordinated and powerless.

Exercise 11 Breathing (4)

Push and pull with resistance – (adapted from an exercise by Peter Adegboyega Badejo).[7]

1   Stand with feet apart, left leg forward and foot pointing front, right leg behind and right foot at a right angle to left foot (see Figure 1.6). Raise the right hand to the ceiling behind you. Take a breath in.

2   Breathe out while pushing forward over the left foot with both the pelvis and the right hand as if pushing with great resistance. It is vital to push with the pelvis or you will finish leaning forward and have less force in the hand.

3   Breathe in and lead with the pelvis back, pulling the hand in to the side of the body, as if pulling something very heavy (i.e. with considerable resistance).

7 Peter Badejo is a Yoruba performer and trainer of performers, resident in the UK. His wide knowledge of west African performance styles has been critical to the development of the intercultural debate in Britain, and to the author's understanding.

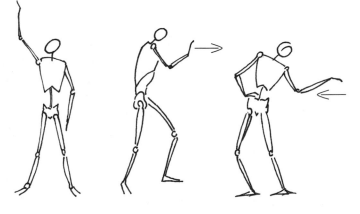

starting position   the push forward   the pull back

Figure 1.6 Breathing (4)

4   Breathe out and lead with the pelvis and hand to push forward as in 2 (above).

5.   Breathe in as, with no resistance, you swing the hand freely back to your starting position.

Repeat, feeling how the long breath can find the force in the action and how the 'breathing centre' pushes and pulls the whole body.

Repeat on the other side.

Now we are beginning to understand energy as effort which is the basis of many mimetic arts from the 'white mime' of Marcel Marceau to the physical suggestion of groups like Théâtre de Complicité. Even the simple illusion of making a stage prop seem heavy requires knowledge which starts here.

BREATHING, CENTRED FOR ENERGY – JUMPS

With the flow of breath centred, and its energy ready for use, you will already feel a latent power within you, waiting to be released. These jumps are a simple way of seeing how the breath can translate into action.

THE JUMPS

8 A participant in an actors' workshop who was also a basketball player reported how these exercises had helped him understand the leap for the basket, and had considerably improved it.

The extraordinary thing to discover through these exercises is that by using the breath, jumping becomes easier. It seems to flow, without stress on the leg muscles, and the jumps can be instantaneous without any initial preparation. Normally, for example, you have to drop down to activate the spring. This tells everyone you are about to jump. With the correct breathing the jump can be totally unannounced, even come as a surprise.[8]

Exercise 12 Straight jump

Stand in the centred position. Take a deep breath to the abdomen. Feel the gathered energy – as if this breath 'charges' your power-centre, and feel that this gives potential for a multitude of movements. Breathe out.

Breathe in again. On the next outward breath feel as if the energy flows straight down the legs and shoots you into the air. Land softly in the centred position without 'bounce' (like a cat, ready to move off at once in full control of your energy).

Practise this until you can shoot upwards at the slightest impulse. It is important to keep the spine vertical, and the knees unlocked so that there is no imbalance or jolt on landing.

Exercise 13 Half-turn jump

As above but now execute a half-turn as you jump on the outward breath, as if when 'en-garde' you suddenly hear a sound from behind and instantly leap round to face it.

Exercise 14 Full-turn jump

As above but now execute a full-turn to land back in your original position. This may seem to be beyond possibility but in fact almost everyone I have led through this exercise has achieved it as soon as they trust the 'explosion' of the breathing.

Again it is vital to maintain a straight spine. It is the axis around which you turn. If not you spin off into space!

Also be aware that you must jump from both feet simultaneously or you are thrown off your central axis. In fact this exercise is also an excellent device to discover your vertical axis, and how to hold it as a constant in all your work.

Extension

To find the moment.

Between any two (or more) people there is a right moment for a gesture, a movement, a word, etc. which is directly linked to the attainment of the tension between the performers. It is not a moment which can be counted, it is the 'now' that has to be found, and which gives tension and credibility to your work.

9 Jacques Lecoq searched long to establish such moments, asking his students 'not to send a telegram' (i.e. a visible sign) that they were about to do something, but to find the inner energy out of which it could spring. Such correct 'timing' is at the base of a feeling of reality in the moment; to move, to embrace, to hit or to deliver a line of text.

1   Two partners in centred positions. Make eye contact with your partner. Breathe in. Together count 1-2-3 and you both jump with a full-turn to land back in eye contact. This is relatively easy.

2   As above but with no counting. Find the moment from sensing the preparedness of the other. This is the moment when your energies become focused and at their optimum level to interact. Then jump together. Do not give a signal, a nod, a leg-dip, etc. and do not lead. There is no leader. Work at it until you achieve that moment together. Difficult at first but magic when it comes.[9]

RESISTANCE

With the energy awakened and put into action, it is important to use it in a way which is not wasteful. If the energy is just thrown around and out of the body it is gone. If it is kept under control, retained in the body, the performer has latent power, useable power.

This is seen at perhaps its most extreme in Japanese Noh Theatre but is applicable to the smallest, simplest gesture.

The quality of 'resistance' gives an exciting tension to any movement. It is as if the energy is not just running out of the body, but is used very deliberately, the performer is sensed to have 'intention'. Having intention in a movement gives credibility and engages the audience in what will happen.

Resistance is achieved at the moment a force is running in one direction in the body and another force is holding that same movement back. It is like pushing through a viscous liquid, but of course you are really resisting your own movement by finding the muscles to execute the movement and those opposing muscles which will hold that movement back and stop it moving so fast.

We have already begun to feel this in Breathing (4) above.

Exercise 15 The resisting walk

Work with a partner. Face your partner with bent knees and a low centre. One partner places a hand on the chest of the other with considerable pressure. The other partner matches the energy to prevent being pushed backwards. At this point you have equal energies – 50 per cent each. You can increase the push against each other and, as long as this is equal, you will remain static, in that apparent contradiction of having maximum energy but no movement, stillness containing power!

When the resisting partner yields very slightly the energy proportion shifts to 51 per cent against 49 per cent and of course you begin to move towards the weaker side. The first partner maintains the resistance and moves slowly backwards, keeping the same pressure through the hand. Both move in a smooth, low centred line. The second partner, moving forwards, feels both forces, the forward one being slightly more than that pushing back.

Initially there will be a tendency to move jerkily from foot to foot, stopping at the end of each step. If the breathing is kept constant and the weight centred, a smooth firm line can be obtained. If the foot slides along the floor, passes close to the other foot and forward for the exchange of weight the walk becomes easier and is close to the basic Noh Theatre walk.

Be sure to move from the centre (the hips) and not to lean on your partner with the chest ahead of the pelvis. You should be in a position that, should your partner remove the hand, you would remain vertical (but move a lot faster). Establishing the hips as the source of energy is close to the Japanese physical aesthetic where the term ko-shi means both 'hips' and 'energy'.

When the partner allows the resisting push to become equal to the forward push you will come to a standstill (a stop is thus a position with doubled energy, one in each direction), and by increasing the resistance to be stronger than the push forward the movement will be reversed.

Move backwards and forwards several times until it is smooth.

Exercise 16 Creating your own resistance

Now undertake exactly the same exercise BUT keep a gap of about 15 centimetres between one partner's hand and the other partner's chest. Go through the same exercise trying to feel the same resistance between hand and chest as if it were in contact. The partner's hand serves as a reminder of what external opposing force is like.

Of course the body is now trying to create both the push forward and the (opposing) resistance within it. When both forces are equal in you there is a standstill. When the push forward begins to exceed the resisting force within you, even 51 per cent–49 per cent, movement begins. The whole body is engaged in this push but the flow of energy must not block in the shoulders or neck to show as excess tension. Neither must the breathing stop – it must flow to 'power' the movement. And the motor of the movement is the base of the spine and the abdomen – your centre.

Exercise 17 Taking your resistance into space

Stand at a considerable distance from your partner. If in a group two lines can be formed, at least 5 metres apart. One line is the 'movers', one is the 'resisters'. The resisting partner holds up one hand as if to stop your movement. You move slowly, in the same manner as above, towards that hand, feeling the resistance growing, compressing, as you approach it. Repeat, exchanging roles with your partner.

Having created the resistance in your body you can now move anywhere without your partner. Feel as if the resistance is always present and your walk will become much more alert and in control. With such control you can stop the walk at any point. Unlike normal walking, where you are constantly losing balance, and therefore control, this is in a state of constant control.

Exercise 18 Resistance with sticks

This extends the last exercise but gives a wider body range to the resistance. It also increases the feeling that the space between bodies is the source of resistance. Sticks should only be used after time taken to become confident with throwing the stick. A stick should always be thrown to land in the partner's hand: throw it to them not at them!

A stick of approximately 1.5m is used, and is placed between the chests of two partners. By putting pressure equally on the stick (50 per cent– 50 per cent) it can be held in position (see Figure 1.7).

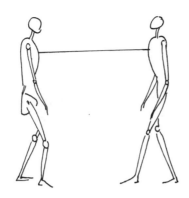

Figure 1.7 Chest to chest

Start to move slowly and smoothly holding the stick in position with the pressure of your bodies. It must not slip and any movement forward should be met with considerable resistance (e.g. 60 per cent–40 per cent). To stop a person moving backwards you need only to increase the resistance to equal that of the force moving forward. By the other person decreasing the pressure the movement is reversed. Maintain eye contact with your partner, do not look at the stick.

Try to find a smooth progress without one of the partners always leading, and without dropping the stick.

When this works smoothly change the stick position on the body. First abdomen to abdomen then shoulder to shoulder, forehead to forehead with extra concentration so that the stick does not slip (see Figures 1.8, 1.9 and 1.10). And for the ambitious turn around and try back of the neck to back of the neck!

Then try the stick between unlike places, e.g. shoulder to abdomen, thigh to chest, etc.

When these are running smoothly a leader should walk through the room and gently remove the stick from between the bodies. Each pair then continues exactly as if the stick were still there, creating the same resistance in their own bodies. Try with each of the positions you tried with the stick. (I have even seen it tried facing away from each other – a fascinating attempt to feel the distance and pressure of another person without looking.) Your body is now moving with resistance but freely in a slow interactive playfulness.[10]

10 In all of these attempts keeping a low centre and deep smooth breathing will help the movement come alive and stay smooth and strong.

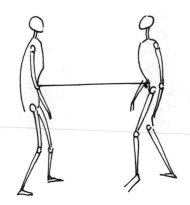

Figure 1.8 Abdomen to abdomen

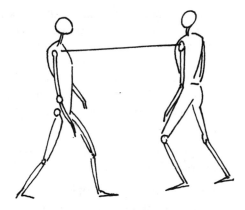

Figure 1.9 Shoulder to shoulder

Figure 1.10 Forehead to forehead

Extension

When the above stage is reached you can extend the image. Leaving your partner, move slowly on a deep centre and without jolts. Move in any direction, backwards, forwards, sideways, but imagine and feel the presence and resistance of a stick resisting you from whichever direction you choose as if the whole of space is exerting a resistance on you, or as if you are exerting resistance on the whole space. Feel that you must make a conscious decision to engage the body with the space. Each movement is 'decided' and has intention.[11]

STATES AND ENERGIES WITHIN THE BREATHING

Developing from the initial breathing exercises we can define four basic states:

- ACTIVE breathing
  Breathing in
  Breathing out
- PASSIVE breathing
  Breathing held in (i.e. breathe in, then hold it in)
  Breathing held out (i.e. breathe out all air, then hold it out).

It is worth spending some time trying each of these states while executing a tough physical action, e.g. lifting a partner or pushing against a wall, to discover the different effect these states have on action. Try to make the action identical on each breathing state and check the results.

With very few exceptions the following are the conclusions:

- The weakest   –   Passive, held out
- Weak   –   Active, breathing in
- Limited strength   –   Passive, held in
- Strongest   –   Active, breathing out.

There is sometimes contention as to which of the last two is really strongest.

In fact both have strength. The passive held-in breath is indeed very strong for a short time (a weight-lifter usually uses this held

11 To get maximum control it is necessary to move from the groin – moving the legs without the upper body swaying from the vertical with each step. Leg swings will help ease this joint. This differentiation of upper and lower body at the groin is seen in many traditional forms, Noh, Kabuki, Kathakali, Beijing Opera. It is very important to master it as it leaves the upper body clear and free whilst moving – clear for reaction and expression as character work is developed.

breath for 'snatch' lifting), but cannot be repeated more than a few times. On the other hand the active breathing-out allows you to repeat an action time and time again. Loading sacks, or wielding a sledge-hammer would automatically need this breathing. Try it and see.

As for the weaker breathings it is of course contradictory to give out energy whilst taking energy in, so that breathing in will not work for strong actions – it is good for preparatory movements, like the back-swing before a throw.

And the passive, held-out breath is at the end of the 'giving out' and before taking in energy, so there is no energy left to work with.

These different states of breathing can be of great use to us.

First, in better executing any movement, be it lifting, chopping or performing an acrobatic roll (try such rolls on different breathing states, but be careful, the different states produce unexpected results.)

Second, in creating the illusion of effort on stage, in mime or any other image-making. (And note that comedy often relies on creating the 'wrong', i.e. opposite, effect. Try for example lifting, or miming lifting, weights on the passive held-out breath, and you are in the world of Buster Keaton.)

Third, and most important for the actor, these different types of breathing create different states of feeling and emotion in us by a psycho-physical process.

Try these to see (and think of more yourselves).

Exercise 19 Breathing and gesture

Standing with feet slightly apart, make the simple gesture of raising the right hand straight up as if signalling to someone.

Now try the gesture four times on each of the following:

- On an inward breath
- On an outward breath
- On a passive held-in breath
- On a passive held-out breath.

You will find the different breathing gives a very different dynamic to each movement. Moreover this dynamic recalls to the body a state of feeling and emotion. Try it before reading the section below.

The four states can be generalised as follows, but each person will find their own spontaneous associations from trying it out and from observing others:

- Breathing in on the signal: welcoming someone, seeing someone arrive, contentment.

- Breathing out on the signal: saying goodbye, seeing someone leave, the end of something, sadness

- Held-in breath on the signal: surprise, shock at suddenly seeing someone or thinking you saw someone.

- Held-out breath on the signal: powerlessness, depression, listlessness, beyond hope.

Now try the same series of breathing states:

- walking to a partner and shaking hands

- facing a partner and sitting together/rising together

- entering a room

- reaching to caress someone.

And, having assimilated these differences, play with them, with or without a partner, so that every move toward or away from a person or an object can be played through the breathing. Move through the room reacting to different people and features with the breathing. A complete scene can be played through the breathing, echoing each change, each new stimulus.

This is a deep and fascinating way to bring your movement to life, and can be further deepened by changing the speed of each breath.

Some examples of this would be:

1 Try very fast, very shallow breathing; move with it through the room. Note the associations and feelings within the body, the way you meet other people and the emotional states which it reminds you of.

2 Try a 'broken' inward breath, i.e. dividing the inward breath into 3 or 4, followed by a slow exhalation. Set it as a pattern, move with it. What does it awaken in you?

3   Try a more complex pattern, e.g. fast inward breath, long held-in breath and outward breath broken into three slow phases. Set the pattern, move with it and observe the associations.

There are many more permutations, which you can work out and try.

The result of this is to demonstrate the deep and intimate link between breathing, action and associative feeling.

Such devices must finally be absorbed into the actor's total vocabulary but can be used quite consciously in finding a character (what is his/her principal breathing state and speed?), to find a 'moment' (which breathing best expresses it?), etc. In an extension of the above examples it is good to expand your knowledge of the breathing-character link like this:

Character through breathing

Work in twos.

One of you invents a breathing pattern. Then teach it to your partner. When it is learned let your partner go into the space and react with objects (tables, chairs, cups, newspapers) to manipulate. Observe what type of character emerges.

ENERGY AND EYES

There is very little which is more important to the performer than the eyes. If the rest of the body is alive and active but the eyes are dead, the effect is that of an automaton.

And in a still body the eyes, if they are alive, can draw our attention magnetically.

It is not always a question of having big eyes, or of stretching your eyes wide. It is the finding of a lively intensity, which seems both to project energy outwards like a beam and to receive information inwards like a radar-scanner.

Once while working with a particularly good group of performers in London, all from different backgrounds and disciplines, and working hard towards presence and alertness, we were visited by a delegation of Chinese actors and theatre-teachers. They watched our training and were very impressed but they said, 'Their eyes are dead'.

Admittedly seeing the 'bright-face' (Xie-Yi) movement which punctuates the Beijing Opera's actions with piercing eyes is an extreme example, but it is part of what makes this form so eminently watchable, even when the language and culturally determined gestures are not completely understood.

Similarly the Kathakali actor trains for years to have an astonishing mobility of the eyeballs and of the muscles surrounding the eyes. Within the full Kathakali make-up the eyes need to stand out, but in the form of 'Chulliyatam' (performances without costumes and make-up), the eyes are tremendously live and mobile expressers of any nuance of emotion.

Alas in the western theatre, naturalism and realism have killed off this heightened use of the body's most expressive organ. We are reduced to admiring the 'huge eyes' of stage beauties, or the 'mysterious eyes' of a 'cool' film star – not the flexible, potentially ever-changing eyes which could be developed by every performer.

Exercise 20 Preparing the eyes

We have already mentioned that to think of the eyes as an extension of the spine helps link them into our whole system of energy and some of the Kathakali training exercises for the eyes are excellent preparation.

Hold the eyelids back as far as possible with the thumb and fore-finger of each hand while the eyeballs work as smoothly as possible.

Let the eyes describe circles, slowly at first then faster. Then progress to vertical up and down movements, then horizontal side to side movements, and finally figures of eight or 'Z' shapes.

The eyes will tend to jump from point to point rather than trace a smooth line at first. Check with a partner, and even let your partner trace the shape with a finger that you can follow, before you try it again alone.

The eyes will be very tired when you first do this. An excellent way of relaxing them is to rub the palms of your hands together vigorously until they are quite warm, and then press them into the eyes – you will feel the heat transfer and relax the eye muscles. Draw the hands from the inside to the outside. Repeat several times.[12]

12 In traditional Kathakali training this process is aided by putting oil into the eyes (I have seen ghee used). It stops the membranes drying out when the eyes are held open, thus allowing greater mobility. It also blurs the vision and the eyes are less likely to 'stop' on distinct objects. Oil should not be used in eye exercises undertaken without supervision.

In the same way that we were training the energy to explode and contract through breathing, try the same with the eyes. Practise closing the eyes as tight as possible and then instantly opening them as wide as possible, focusing on a different point in the space each time in a single, powerful action. First slowly, then accelerating. Be careful that you are only opening the eyes wide and not furrowing the forehead and raising the eyebrows, which would give a very different message.

Actors from the Beijing Opera taught us the following exercise to keep the eyes constantly alert in all states. Establish three positions of the eyes:

1 very open eyes
2 medium-open eyes
3 narrowed eyes.

Ensure that you have all the energy from the above exercise in position 1 then change to position 2 and keep the same energy; then change to position 3 keeping the same energy. The Chinese actors then had us walking around the room, shouting the numbers on which we had to change eye position but not the intensity of the energy in the eyes.

FOCUSING AND CREATING SPACE

To find and create space with eyes.

Exercise 21 Eye information

Move around the room. Start to feel the eyes as receivers of information, and deciders of direction. Fix a point with the eyes, move towards it, stop, fix another point, move straight towards it, then another and another. Start with points at eye level, then include higher and lower points, including points on the ceiling and the floor. The eyes are leading. Try fixing a point and moving away from it, or sideways towards or away from it. Keep moving so the whole room is pulling or repelling you through the information determined by the eyes.

Exercise 22 Close space

Hold a hand in front of the face as close as possible while still keeping it in focus. Start walking while only looking at the hand. Feel the closeness of the space you are creating. There is enough peripheral vision to be able to move around quite freely, even running, and still avoid collisions.

Exercise 23 Far space

Stop in the same position, hand in front of the face. As you lower the hand let the eyes focus further and further away to a horizon some 10 kilometres distant. For this you will have to look through the walls of whichever room you are in. This may seem difficult at first but by concentrating on a mental image of a horizon (at the sea-shore, from a hill-top, etc.), it is soon possible. Feel how the body reacts to this state. There is a feeling of the energy streaming out to the horizon and the body involuntarily changes its posture, tending upwards and outwards. Moreover you will automatically find that there is no need to move rapidly. A calm slow walk is enough, looking all around the 360 degrees.

By mastering this you are able to begin what is a vital yet unregarded area of acting, you can transcend the shape and limitation of your theatre-space and create new spaces for your action and thus for your audience. Creating a larger, or smaller, space than your actual stage is a fundamental part of taking your audience on its journey of the imagination.

Change rapidly between the very close and very distant eye space. Feel how the body changes. Feel how your thoughts and associations change with each.

Exercise 24 Eye contacts

A route to pre-expressive playfulness.

These are perhaps the most important exercises to develop a sense of playfulness and then creativity – they stress the eyes' ability to concentrate the body and to transmit and receive a multitude of signals.

This pre-expressive playfulness is a state of preparedness which is very important in improvisation. It allows impulses to emerge freely from the moment, without the inner 'censor' voice telling you if it is good or bad. It is close to the Indian concept of creativity through *Anand* (joy), or Jean-Louis Barrault's desire that his actors should be like young kittens which can play with total spontaneity and involvement, then break off from the play just as totally.

Start by walking around the space without looking at anyone. Just let the eyes wander without specific focus.

Stage 1 – Flash contact

As you pass someone in the group make a very short eye contact and immediately break it. It should take only the time to establish the eye contact – a 'flash' of two sets of eyes meeting, and instantly focusing. You lock into the eye contact and then immediately break it. Keep moving, do not stop for the eye contact.

Stage 2 – Two-second contact

The group continues walking at random in all directions. As you pass someone make eye contact with them and let it last for a 2 second count. Then break it and continue. Repeat this many times. Allow this contact to affect the way you move. With each new contact this will be different. It may pull you towards the other person, it may slow you down or speed you up but don't stop. By stopping you will freeze a moment and block any other reaction. By keeping moving you can let your movement, rhythm and body language be affected.

When this is established play with the way you break the eye contact. How you break it by looking away downwards, upwards or sideways will give quite different feelings, affecting your status in relation to the other.

Stage 3 – Five-second contact

As above but let the contact last a full 5 seconds and slow without stopping. Of course this changes the relationship. You cannot just walk past. You will have either to change the direction of your walk or turn your body as you pass. Feel this effect on yourself. The eye contact is like an elastic between you. It can come very close or stretch across the space. It can take bodies high or low. This is why we don't stop. By continuing we test the elasticity of the eye contact. Let the speed and dynamic vary with each contact. It is as if each contact is a meeting of magnets, some are strong some weak, some attract and some repel.

Stage 4 – Ten-second contact

The same as stage 3 but with a contact of 10 seconds. The movements through the space become vital. Now you need not be close to each other, but can stretch the eye contact across the room. Keep it just as strong over this distance.

Stage 5 – Thirty-second play

The same again but a 30 second eye contact. At this stage the messages in the eye contact become essential. It is not just meeting and parting. It is spending time together and the sense of play between you can be unleashed.

Enjoy the movements which flow from the contact. Allow them to develop with no pre-planning. Advancing, retreating, stretching apart, rushing together, on the ground, in the air, slow and fast. You can be a receiver and a suggester so there is a constant flow of impulses between you, and not one leader. If a pattern of movement, or a rhythm emerges then allow yourself to let it develop. Be alert and let new situations enter the play.

Stage 6 – Eye play with stops

Now that the play element has developed, each contact can last as long as the director/teacher sees fit – 2 or 3 minutes at least. The playfulness will allow moods and rhythms to change constantly, an ever varying set of relationships, moods and dynamics.

And now the 'stop' can be introduced. The stop should not be a relaxation but a double energy 'hold' (your first movement held by an equal opposite force) from which the next movement naturally emerges.

Stage 7 – Eye play with breaks

Continue the game, including the stops, but for a very brief instant you can look away and break the eye contact; then snap back into it with extra energy and continue. The breaks can be during a movement or during a stop.

We are searching for the playfulness between us. There is no given character or situation, and yet through reaching to this level of play, relationships, situations, status and power structures all emerge flowing one into the other. Allow it to happen and it will come remarkably alive with that freshness we seek for all our theatre work.

These exercises, when adapted, can become the basis for a lot of detailed improvisation work (see Chapter 4).

ENERGY IN KNEELING AND SITTING

Exercise 25 Strong breathing, strong centre, strong presence

Adapted and developed from a Japanese Kabuki exercise brought to my training by a Swiss actress!

This is an excellent, slow way to generate and control centred energy in a simple structured sequence. There is a base position, kneeling, with a strong centred feeling as shown in Figure 1.11. The arms are slightly lifted to increase the feeling of the body's size. The back is straight.

From here the body moves to six different positions. Each move is preceded by a still phase for breathing in over 4 counts. The movement is executed on, and in exactly the length of, the outward breath of 4 counts. For another 4 counts you hold that position and take an inward breath. Over 4 more counts you breathe out and return to your base position.

It is vital to start and control each movement from the centre. Feel it like a heavy iron ball in the pelvis to be lifted and brought down gently in a straight line. For example, be careful in the first movement

Figure 1.11 Base position

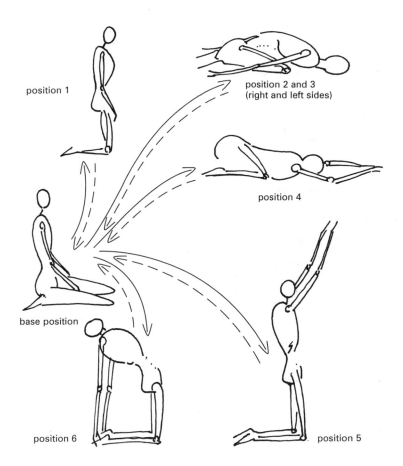

position 1

position 2 and 3
(right and left sides)

position 4

base position

position 6

position 5

Figure 1.12 Kneeling positions

not to bend the body forward but to rise vertically from the kneeling position.

Base to position 1

4 beats – base position – breathe in

4 beats – rise to full kneel – breathing out

4 beats – stay there – breathe in

4 beats – descend to base position – breathing out

(repeat 4 times)

Base to position 2

4 beats – base position – breathe in

4 beats – stretch the back forward until the right cheek touches the floor – breathing out

4 beats – stay there – breathe in

4 beats – draw back to base position – breathing out

(repeat 4 times)

Base to position 3

As for position 2 with left cheek to floor

(repeat 4 times)

Base to position 4

4 beats – base position – breathe in

4 beats – stretch spine and arms forward on the floor in front of you as far as possible – breathing out

4 beats – stay there – breathe in

4 beats – draw back to base position – breathing out

(repeat 4 times)

Base to position 5

4 beats – base position – breathe in

4 beats – rise vertically upwards, arms stretching above the head, eyes following hands – breathing out

4 beats – stay there – breathe in

4 beats – descend to base position – breathing out

(repeat 4 times)

Base to position 6

4 beats – base position – breathe in

4 beats – lift pelvis forward and bend fully back until hands touch the heels – breathing out

4 beats – stay in position – breathe in

4 beats – lower the pelvis back to base position – breathing out

(repeat 4 times)

Having completed this cycle, repeat it on a 2 beat base (2 for each in-breath, 2 for each out-breath, moving to each position only 2 times).

Then do the complete cycle on a 1 beat base (1 for the in-breaths, 1 for the out-breaths, moving to each position once only).

This is a great strengthening exercise but may be difficult at first. If the kneeling is uncomfortable on a wooden floor, try using a mat or small pad. When you can work the 4 beat cycle as described, extend the cycle to 8 beats on each breath and repeat each movement 8 times.

Exercise 26 Power standing, power sitting

Return to the 4 beat cycle:

4 beats – base position – breathe in

4 beats – rise to a standing position (no hands), lifting the back vertically – breathing out – arrive on fourth beat

4 beats – stay standing – breathing in

4 beats – lower the body to the base position – breathing out, holding the back vertical throughout

Then, using the same breathing/action pattern on 4 beats, stand and sit trying all the following sitting positions. The centre powers each action and the back stays vertical, giving the body a strong sense of presence:

1   Sit, sliding the left foot behind the right leg in a cross-legged sit, the right knee stays high. The left knee must have crossed behind the right knee before the weight descends. Stand, keeping the back straight as you rise (Figure 1.13).

2   Sit, right foot behind left leg into cross-legged sit, left knee stays high. Stand, keeping the back straight as you rise.

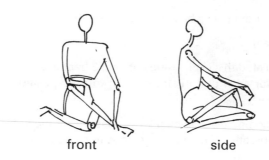

front   side

Figure 1.13 Sitting position (1)

3   Slide the right foot in front of the left leg to descend into a cross-legged sit. Stand, keeping the back straight as you rise (Figure 1.14).

4   Slide the left foot in front of the right leg to descend into a cross-legged sit. Stand, keeping the back straight as you rise.

5   Right leg back to a one-knee kneel. Stand, keeping the back straight as you rise.

6   Left leg back to a one-knee kneel. Stand, keeping the back straight as you rise (Figure 1.15).

Now, abandon the counted breathing but not the feeling of it. Move about the room, practise going into each of these sits, then repeat, meeting people with different sits at different speeds.

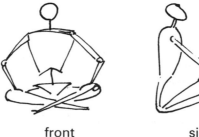

front   side

Figure 1.14 Sitting position (3)

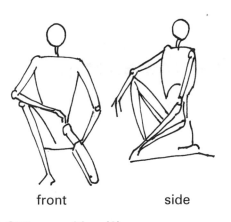

front   side

Figure 1.15 Sitting position (6)

The ability to sit and stand with this powerful vertical movement from the centre gives great strength and dominance to a character. It leaves the upper body free from having to bend or support itself, so that any small gesture or expression can be clearly read.

This quality is highly visible in Noh Theatre. It has been linked to the way a samurai would move, ever ready to draw a sword, and anyone who has seen Kurosawa's film *Ran* must have seen this strength in the principal female character.

Kanhailal Singh, the Manipuri theatre director, has developed similar exercises to give his actors control of space and situation. He draws from the Manipuri martial arts form, Thang Tha.

Sitting and standing are such basic movements, but are normally executed in a surprisingly clumsy, weak manner which robs us of the moments of strength.

2   Using the energy

'Slowly it becomes acting.'
(Ramnath on experiencing these exercises during initial training
of actors for the Rangayana company in Karnataka, India)

Having found ways of generating and gathering the energy needed
for our basic presence, let us look at the first ways of letting that
energy flow out through the body expressively.

Many of these ways will throw up associations, memories and
feelings because they are archetypical or because they recall
situations we have experienced. It is vital that we do not block these
associations because they give life to our actions. It is equally vital
that we do not try to 'act them out'. Just let them enter the work
you are doing as if they are 'colouring' it. Note them, for they are
increasing your vocabulary.

They are also offering you an approach to character and to
situation. It is the subtle changes in energy concentrated in different
parts of the body, or the energy flowing at different speeds and
different directions which change the actor's neutral, 'latent', body
to create a new being or a new mood.

You will look at the energy in terms of:

- Opening and closing
- Geometric and organic
- The seven levels of tension
- Symmetry and asymmetry (balance and counter-direction)
- Body parts and body language
- Contradiction
- Percentage dimensions (expansion and contraction)
- Element identification.

OPENING AND CLOSING

In the simplest mode the energy flows outwards from the centre of the body to the extremities and beyond, and then flows back to the centre. It flows in and out.

Many have identified this basic ebb and flow and have given it illustrative names like 'scattering and gathering', 'giving and taking', 'sowing and harvesting', but we are essentially talking about OPENING AND CLOSING THE BODY.

Following this definition any movement or position can be seen as opening or closing (or as opened or closed), with some more complex movements having interesting contradictions where one part of the body is opening, and another part is closing (see also the section on Contradiction).

It must be stressed that as we start to play with these two elements neither is better nor worse than the other – they are different states and both are a necessary part of our existence and of our expression.

So let us start to understand this:

Exercise 27 Beyond the body

Stand with the feet slightly apart and shake the hands vigorously until they are relaxed and feel like rubber. When you stop, spread the hands out in front of you, the fingers fanned out wide. You may feel a tingling sensation in the tips of the fingers as if the energy has been awakened there.

Then, on a long outward breath, stretch the arms forward, up to above the head, over to each side, then down, pointing to the floor. Then draw them up towards your centre with a deep inward breath. Shake them again and repeat. Feel the energy reaching out through the fingers into the space, as if the fingers had elongated to touch the ceiling and walls.

As you start to feel this, leave out the hand-shaking and just bring the hands up into tight, closed fists in front of your chest on the inward breath, and shoot them open, fingers stretched out and up, as you breathe out.

This gives a strong image in the closed hands of gathering energy, and in the open hands of exploding the energy outwards. Try

49

shooting the energy out through the hands to a specific point, to a person, to a part of a person.

Exercise 28 The outward–inward flow

Start again with the hands. Hold them open, palm forward, at about shoulder height.

Slowly roll the fingers, one by one, into a closed fist, starting with the little finger, ending with the thumb.

Then roll them open in the same order to a broad stretched hand.

Repeat several times. Then add a wrist movement; towards the body on the closing (inward) roll, and away from the body on the opening (outward) roll. Repeat a few times.

Then add the forearm to this opening and closing (the elbow stays as a fixed point). Now add movement in the whole arm. You are still starting with the fingers but the closing leads the whole arm into the abdomen and the opening takes it out to a full stretch.

Finally, take the hand-wrist-arm into a closing body to the extreme of a low crouch. As you open, stretch the body up and out to its widest dimensions. The ebb and flow has entered the whole body.

Exercise 29 The closed body

Now stop in the fully closed position (see Figure 2.1). Allow yourself any associations which come to you through being in this position. Move around the room, still in this very closed position. Notice how you move, with what rhythm, with what relationship to the room and to other people. What feelings emerge through this movement? Who are you when you are like this?

Exercise 30 The open body

Now open the body fully, expanding outwards from the centre, letting the energy reach right to the fingertips (see Figure 2.1). Walk in this position. It may seem strange at first to be so unprotected,

closed – protective/secretive   open – generous/vulnerable

Figure 2.1 The closed body and the open body

so vulnerable, and to hold this position while in a space with several others. This position would be much more natural if you were alone in a big space, or were the only person in this position in front of others who were not. Again allow any associations to emerge. Ask yourself who you become in this position.

Having felt these two positions and their essentially different flows of energy we can extend them as follows.

Exercise 31 The closing body

The closed position is essentially passive. To make it active stay in this position, move around, and with hands and arms, add closing movements to it, as if more and more is being gathered into the centre. Again as you move around notice how you react to the space and to other people. Let it colour the way you move. You will now be in the world of gathering, stealing, bringing into a very protected centre. This could be a mean, covetous thief, but equally a protective mother gathering food for a child. Or again it could be nursing a deep pain in the abdomen and containing the body's forces to deal with it.

Exercise 32 The opening body

The opposite active phase is opening. Take the open extended position and add to it opening gestures with arms and hands, constantly giving more and more outwards. Move and associate. This is a flow of generosity, distributing blessings or money or hopes or promises. Your associations will colour the movement. And notice how you react, when moving around, to other people engaged in the same movements. So much giving in one space!

These two extremes can be experienced by a simple technical change of body from one to the other. However, more realisation of the life within them can be felt by finding a stimulus for the change. When you are in one position moving around, stop – pick something to concentrate on (it could be looking at someone or something or listening to a noise) and use this stimulus to inspire and begin the change.

You will find that your attitude to this stimulus-point alters during the change of position. By taking the change slowly you can start to feel the details of this. *As in many dramatic situations it is the process of changing which is often more interesting than the beginning or end states.*

Now move around the room and meet people. At each meeting find something in that person to stimulate a change from one position to the other (a look in their eyes, a piece of jewellery, the colour of their clothes, etc.). Sometimes you will meet a partner in the same extreme and you will both be changing together. At other times you will meet someone of the opposite extreme. This is already a more interesting dramatic situation since there is an imbalance between you. The 'exchange' of positions is an interesting game (we are in the area of the doctor who becomes patient, servant who becomes master, etc., much loved by playwrights).

Exercise 33 Opening and closing gestures

Only now do we start talking of gestures. Only when the body is well involved in action. There is a tendency for actors to rely on gestures without the body. This can lead to very external acting – still, unexpressive bodies with wild, windmill actions. Although this might be useful in comic situations, it normally looks artificial and dishonest.

Only where a gesture is rooted in the dynamic body does it appear honest.

With this in mind explore the field of opening gestures (see Figure 2.2). Start with large giving and scattering gestures, then explore medium and small gestures still with the emphasis on the opening, the flow of energy outwards from the centre through the body. Some of these may be gestures you use every day or that you have seen.

When you are in the flow of these, which at first is quite technical, start directing them towards someone who is across the room from you. Develop a 'gesture conversation' with them but only on opening gestures. Note the kind of mood which emerges from this.

Now develop the reverse, concentrating on closing gestures, coming in towards you (see Figure 2.2). Start with large gestures. Then explore smaller ones. Then direct them towards a partner,

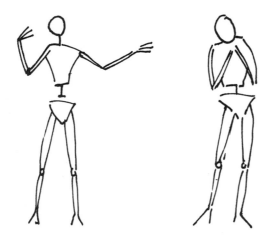

Figure 2.2 Opening and closing gestures

noting the mood of the 'conversation' of gestures. How does it differ from the mood of the opening gestures?

In general terms the opening gestures will be trying to convince the other person, to give them your ideas, or you will be concerned about the other person. The closing gestures will be concentrating on you, your problems, your importance.

To put this into practice try these short improvisations:

- Deliver a political/election speech to a crowd of 10,000 using only outward gestures.

- Deliver one with only inward gestures.

Time and time again (but with great variety) the outward ones are promises of what will be done for the listeners – you the people!

The inward ones are 'Choose me! I am the one for you'.

Of course we normally mix both dynamics to make different types of points (try it!). Observe people around you, almost all characters will have one of these dynamics predominant.

Try the same political speech, but as if in front of a TV camera, once with opening gestures, once with closing gestures. The 'language' is the same but the scale is different, reduced to perhaps 25 per cent of the former exercise.

Try a market situation (markets are very good places to observe gestures). Try selling something with open gestures. Now try selling the same thing with closed gestures. Note the difference in your 'sales technique'. Use words to help you sell and notice the different kind of words which emerge with each type of gesture.

GEOMETRIC AND ORGANIC

This is another simple division into two ways of using our energy. We have already met this division in the stability exercises, as ways of reacting to an impulse.

The word 'geometric' is used here to describe movements made up of straight lines with a clear division of start – movement – stop – change direction – start – movement – stop – etc.

The word 'organic' is used here to describe continuous flowing movements avoiding straight lines or angles and never stopping.

Using energy 'geometrically' or 'organically' can be experienced in many ways and can produce very different feelings.

Start with walking in the room.

Exercise 34 Geometric and organic walks

Geometric walks

Walk only in straight lines. These can be long or short distances but must be absolutely straight with a strong stop. It is as if you are cutting a line through space.

Turn, start a new line, walk, stop and so on. The pattern in space is of strong, straight lines with sharp angles. The energy stops, starts, stops, starts, and this has a strong effect on you. The walk can be faster or slower but the pattern is the same.

Organic walks

Walk in the space in a continuous curving line. No straight lines. No stops. The curves can be tight or long and can turn on themselves. There is a constant flow which can be faster or slower but can never stop.

Walk for about 1 minute geometrically, then 1 minute organically. Keep changing and feel the difference between the two ways of walking.

When you have changed from one to the other several times, the different dynamics become quite clear, as do the feelings which emerge from them. Initially people feel that the geometric is mechanical or military, and that the organic is pleasurable or 'natural'.

We can deepen our association by extending the walks:

1   Walk geometrically searching the space for someone or something.

2   Walk organically searching the space for someone or something. Notice the different types of searching that emerge.

3   Walk geometrically and try to make contact with each other. Be careful not to bend those straight lines! Notice that real contact cannot be sustained for long, only at stops or intersections of lines.

4   Walk in organic lines and try to make contact. Here, of course, you can adapt your path. You can turn and twist to maintain a contact.

5   Now work with one partner who remains standing still. Think of something quite definite you want to say to them: 'I love you', 'Go to hell', 'You lied to me', etc. Use geometric walks to deliver this phrase.

6   Now try to say the same whilst walking in only organic lines.

Of course what may have seemed mechanical in the geometric dynamic now becomes very useful. It is very direct because it cuts through to a stop, and gives you a strong moment to deliver the line.

On the other hand trying to be direct whilst moving organically is impossible because you have to keep moving and because you have to curve away from your partner. You can never come to that commanding position to deliver the line. (Think of a character who would be like this: never able to deliver a direct line forcefully.)

Each of these dynamics has different qualities. Neither is better nor worse, but each is very useful to our vocabulary of movement.

Work with a partner again, but now both of you are moving. Try some short meetings:

•   geometric meets geometric
•   organic meets organic
•   geometric meets organic.

Keep the meetings short, just the time to say 'Hello, how are you?', 'What are you doing?', etc. Notice what embryonic characters emerge from these simple divisions of line.

Exercise 35 Geometric and organic gestures

As with the last exploration of gesture (opening and closing), this sequence is for you to experience differences, and to relate them to what expression emerges from these differences.

Geometric gestures

Stand relaxed with feet apart. With your right hand, as if holding a piece of chalk to a blackboard, make one clean straight line in any direction. From the end of that line make another in any new direction, and so on. Each line is clean and straight with a definite stop and a change of direction into the next. Short lines, long lines, fast or slow. Then work in three dimensions all around your body. Follow the hand with the eye. Let your breath match the action.

Repeat with the left hand, and feel the type of crisp, stop–start rhythm which emerges.

Now use both hands, sometimes moving them together and sometimes one after the other. Try to avoid symmetrical movements (hands tracing equal shapes on each side of the body) as these have much less tension and dynamism.

Organic gestures

Standing in the same starting position move the right hand in a flowing organic line in the space, curving and never stopping (so never making an angle, never getting to the end of a line). Play with the curves; tight ones, circles, long loops above and around the body. Let the breathing accentuate slight accelerations and decelerations.

Try with the left hand.

Try with both hands, again avoiding symmetry in your gestures.

Now change on a signal between the organic and geometric. Feel what happens to your energy and your associations as you change from geometric to organic. What does it mean in your body?

Towards the expressive

- Begin again with the geometric gestures, using both hands but one after the other. Start directing these straight lines towards someone, away from someone or something, so that each gesture takes a relationship with something, someone or your-self (a command, pointing, blocking, etc.). These can be very small (10 per cent) gestures or broad expansive ones.

- Meet someone else also using these gestures. Feel what kind of relationship develops between you. Try letting sounds come with the gestures – what mood do they reflect?

1 A Chinese parallel: the flow of movement using strong circular (organic) lines is greatly used in Chinese performing arts. Ma Ming Qun of the Beijing Opera Academy taught that straight lines were to be avoided as they were too simple and too small (the shortest distance between two points). Round lines cover more space and fill the stage area more. This is true of Beijing Opera where even the patterns of walking on stage are curved, as well as the gestures. What gives these large gestures their clarity is the typical very strong punctuating stop which 'freezes' each sequence. It is organic followed by geometric.

- Now try exactly the same process with the organic gestures. Start quite abstractly and then relate the curve and direction of the line to someone or something in the room. There may be a tendency to stop at the end of a curve. Resist it – keep going! Add sounds without thinking or planning. Just see what sort of sounds come out.

Now try some very simple verbal exercises with each type of gesture, for example:

- give directions to a partner to get to the railway station
- describe your bedroom
- talk about an ambition.

Allow the type of gesture to influence what you say. Don't fight against the mood your gestures suggest (although that will be an interesting exercise in contradiction later).

Here the geometric line comes into its own. It allows you to make point after point with clear punctuation, although it doesn't allow elaborate embroidery of your thoughts.

The organic keeps going and never allows you to reach the point. Another word, thought, clause tumbles out after the last one as if you are trying to work out an excruciating problem, or trying to find an excuse to avoid embarrassment but never getting to a conclusion.

Again, we normally use a mixture of both dynamics to make different sorts of points, but a character is almost always more of one than the other.

Experiment with a mixture, and with the interesting sequence of organic lines (working out the problem), leading to a geometric stop (finding the solution).[1]

Co-ordination exercise

Try to gesture geometrically with one hand and simultaneously gesture organically with the other. Remember the organic can never stop!

THE SEVEN LEVELS OF TENSION

ENERGY AS TENSION

We talk a lot about tension in the work of the actor. This can be very confusing because we use the word to describe both positive and negative conditions:

- 'There's no tension in it' (meaning there should be)
- 'It's too tense' (meaning it shouldn't be)

Of course even in order to stay standing, a certain amount of tension is needed in the body. To be alert we need a little more tension. However, when too much tension is used it blocks a movement, making it stiff and artificial. Too much tension can also block the flow of breath and voice, making it sound strained.

This scale between total relaxation (lack of tension) and rigidity (from too much tension) is important for us to understand. By looking at it we can see where our own optimum levels of energy lie for most effective acting – and how too much or too little can perhaps guide us to the more extreme characters we may create.

And remember that tension is energy in its flow to the body and parts of the body.

Follow and experience this scale of tensions.

Exercise 36 The levels of tension

Level 1

Try to find your minimum operative tension. Let the head drop, the back bend forward, the arms hang very loose. Even lose the tension necessary to stand still (which requires quite a lot of energy held in the ankles and knees) so that your weight is pulling you forwards, backwards, sideways and you constantly have to save yourself from falling. It is very, very loose.

Once you have found this state and are moving around, try to find any associations to this state. Is it like being extremely tired, extremely drunk, or having been badly beaten?

You will also discover that in this first state, with the head dropped, contact with other people is virtually impossible.

Level 2

Find enough tension in the feet and legs to stop and be still. Add enough tension to let the spine pull up to an upright position BUT not enough to hold the head erect. Let it hang forward or if you lift it there should not be the tension to hold it there; it will fall backward. (The head is very heavy and requires a lot of energy to hold it up!) As you start to move let there be only enough tension for you to carry your weight slowly, upright, in a straight line. The arms still hang very loose.

The feeling is like that of walking in extreme heat, or of walking when recovering from severe illness. What other associations come?

Move around the room exploring this level of tension.

Again the amount of communication with others is very limited because the head is not erect in a giving and receiving position.

Level 3

Stop for a moment in the last tension. Now find just enough tension to raise the head to the vertical position (but not enough to bring mobility to the facial muscles). When walking there should be enough tension to walk steadily in a straight line, to stop, turn and start again.

The feeling of the tension is rather 'grey', as if working on an automatic, pre-programmed path. It is the kind of tension in those who follow the same route to work in a big city every single day, or spend all day walking along corridors or production lines without really being alert but with just enough awareness, for example, not to walk under a bus; enough awareness to recognise other people but not to react to them – only perhaps an automatic handshake with no external expression of feeling.

Move with this tension to explore its possibilities.

Level 4

Stop in level 3 and allow enough tension to rise into the face that the eyes come alive and start looking, the ears start hearing, the nose starts to smell and the mouth to taste. Moreover the skin on the whole body becomes sensitised to temperature, touch, etc.

This means that the senses now lead the movement. React to any sense-stimulus. From a still moment, in which all the senses are awake, pick out one stimulus and follow it, as if asking what it is: 'What did I smell? What did I hear? What did I feel? What did I see, feel, taste, etc.?'

Move towards the source of the stimulus. This can lead you to examine anything, from a light entering through a window, a breeze through the door or the colour on someone's T-shirt, and thus give a good enquiring contact with other people.

Each movement to examine is followed by a stillness to await the next stimulus. Note how much tension you require just to create this alert stillness. It is the kind of tension of a hunted animal, but also of the hunter. It is an alive stillness which is full of latent energy.

Level 5

Stop in level 4. By adding the next tension we go to a state where the senses are still very awake and in control but rather than asking the question 'What is it?', the tension now occupies every muscle to respond to the stimulus and decide to go to it. It is the tension of decision which cuts effectively through the space to get to where has been decided, to do what has been decided by the senses.

It normally works quite fast but can also be slow. It is always strong and effective. What associations does it bring up?

Level 6

So far we have come from too little tension to be effective (levels 1–3), into two very awake and efficient levels (4 and 5), and now we enter the levels where too much tension is present for clear execution of a movement. It starts to block efficiency.

In this level 6 allow even more tension to rise up to the neck and shoulders and down into the hands as if to make a clenched fist.

It is the tension of wanting to do something but then forcing the impulse back – 'I want to hit you but I won't', 'I want to embrace you but it is not allowed'. The tension starts to flow out with the wish and then is blocked in the body when it cannot be followed through.

Move around the room in this feeling, directing your impulses and blocks to points of the room and particularly to other people.

You will feel quite a strain in the neck, shoulders and upper arms as the energy which cannot get out is held there.

Level 7

This is total tension, as much as possible. Stop in level 6 then try to add tension to every muscle in the body from the toes to the face muscles. Add so much tension that movement is virtually impossible because every muscle is blocking every other muscle, a paroxysm.

It affects the feelings because we are almost in a fit; whether of anger, jealousy or fear, it is the most extreme.

THEN

Having passed through all these levels, return to level 1 to relax the body.

Work through these levels two or three times until you can feel the play of the tension in your body.

All these levels can be useful to us in the study of character but for an actor the levels 4 and 5 are those in which we should always be when we approach our work. The questioning and the deciding are our searching and executing levels, essential for our pre-expressive, and later our expressive, work.

They are the starting levels of so many theatre forms, and much of our training in Chapter 1 is to achieve this. If you can maintain this in rehearsal and on stage all your work will become more vivid. Avoid being in that rather anaesthetised state of level 3.

SYMMETRY AND ASYMMETRY (BALANCE AND COUNTER-DIRECTION)

All our initial work was to find the vertical line through the body, and the centre of energy within it. Inherent in this work is a sense of symmetry, so that the starting point for all work is a clear, alive, neutral position.

However, once we start engaging the energy we soon discover that returning to symmetry is a return to a quite passive state, whereas in theatre terms we almost always need an active position. Symmetry is passive because it is in balance and therefore contains no inherent movement. Only when a position contains inherent movement can it naturally lead to something.

By taking an asymmetric position we immediately feel that it contains a potential to move from where it is. And because it is held still, its opposite movement (counter-tension or counter-direction) is also present. The tension between these two provides the contradiction which gives interest and life to a position. There is an interest because there is a question in the movement (will he/she go this way or that?).

This contradiction is the basis for many characters, many dramatic situations and of course many dramas. When there is an imbalance something starts to happen, something starts to move. There is an inherent drama. Whether this is the heightened position of the Beijing Opera or a look over the shoulder while the body stays facing forward, the body is starting to suggest multiple possibilities.

If we return to exercise 4 (the running and dropping into a centred position) we can explore asymmetry by introducing one difference. As soon as you drop from the run into the centred position, move to an asymmetry by pushing the weight off-centre and stop there (see Figure 2.3). There are hundreds of possible positions.

Figure 2.3 Symmetrical and asymmetrical positions

(arrow shows direction of movement, broken arrow shows
counter-direction)

Figure 2.4 Asymmetrical positions

When you stop in such a position feel the inherent direction of movement, and also feel the counter-direction which is holding the position still (see Figure 2.4).

You will soon realise that much more energy is used to hold these positions in balance than for the symmetrical position. In the symmetrical base there is latent energy. Here there is working energy.

2 It is interesting to look at theatre pictures and drawings of the Commedia dell'Arte (Italy), of Balinese Topeng (Indonesia) and of Beijing Opera (China). All three of these very dynamic theatre styles make great use of asymmetric positions.

When you have tried this several times, try it moving around the room and meeting people. As you meet them react by taking an asymmetric position. Notice that a new dynamism enters the relationship because you are holding back the imbalance in the body.[2]

This same principle can be seen, extended, in the Balance and Counter-direction exercises.

Exercise 37 Balance

Start with the basic run, holding a vertical body line. Drop into a centred position and then throw the body into a balance on one leg and hold it (see Figure 2.5).

(arrows show the 'potential falls' being held)

Figure 2.5 Balances

Try this many times. There are many possible positions. You will feel that a great deal of energy is necessary to hold a balance. The fact that it is difficult means that a fall is all the more likely. A balance, therefore, is an exciting position to watch because of this 'danger'. It is also effective because the audience is fascinated that something very strong must have happened to result in the energy stopping in this 'extra-ordinary' position.

While holding the balance learn to feel what is the movement 'held' in the balance. Inevitably this will be a fall from balance, but in which direction? In particular (and this is where you really feel the great amount of energy in use) where is the counter-force which holds you in balance?

Again move around, and on meeting someone (or as a reaction to any other stimulus in the room) stop in a balance position. Feel the amount of held energy between the two of you holding these positions.

You can, of course, use either the held position or its counter-movement to continue out of the balance. From the held position either follow the fall which is held in the balance, or go with the counter-movement which pulls you out of the fall. And then continue to the next meeting.

Exercise 38 Imbalance

Note also that as much as we concentrate on stability and balance as necessities of presence, the opposite is very interesting and highly useable on stage.

Try to stand in a stable position then gently throw yourself off balance, backwards, forwards or sideways just a few steps, then recover, and repeat.

When this is established, try to analyse how it makes you feel.

It can be quite unnerving, for yet again the physical and the psychological are strongly related. It is interesting that we call people 'unbalanced' or 'unstable' when we speak of their psychological condition.

By reproducing the physical state we are reminded of, and start to feel, the psychological state.

It is a quite natural reaction, for example, on receiving bad news, to lose balance and to have to regain it, to reach out and steady yourself. By losing balance such moments are relived, and your link to your vocabulary is fortified.

Exercise 39 Counter-direction

This is an extension of the asymmetry and an excellent way of understanding it more fully.

In a good centred position keep the legs and pelvis facing forward and the arms raised to shoulder level in an open curve. Start to swing the upper body in a spiral to the left and then to the right so that at the end of each swing the spine, shoulders and head have twisted to look as far round behind you as possible (see Figure 2.6).

On each swing breathe out and stop in a still position at one extreme, looking behind you. Breathe in and repeat the swing to the other side.

At the extreme position (the exercise is very good to increase spine mobility) your legs and pelvis are facing front and the arms and head are facing in the opposite direction behind you.

Move around the room. At the slightest impulse drop into this position with both directions strongly evident in the body.

It is as if in your journey something has caught your attention from behind. It is not strong enough to make you turn your whole body, but enough to make you stop and look. There is an inherent question in this position – will you turn back on yourself or will you continue? It is just this question, this inherent drama, which makes the position, and others like it, so interesting.

At first it will tend to be a quite harsh, defensive action, as if afraid, or threatened from behind. However, taken a little more slowly, it can be quite flirtatious, as somebody you have just passed attracts you but you don't want to fully commit yourself (you could still carry on if he/she does not respond!). Or the position could be quietly curious ('What did I just see?').

Try it and see!

Figure 2.6 Counter-direction

BODY PARTS AND BODY LANGUAGE

Every part says something.

3 The concept of neutrality has been deeply researched by Jacques Lecoq at his Paris school. Lecoq achieves this state by use of the neutral mask, a fascinating journey towards a ready stillness, on which a new vocabulary can be constructed. The development of the neutral mask can be traced back to the ground-breaking work in actor training of Jacques Copeau, who was strongly influenced by Japanese performers.

Our neutral stance, in that alive state of neutrality with energy 'ready-to-go', is like a clean canvas for a painter.[3]

Any slight change in that neutral body puts us into a different state, as it will slightly (or considerably) change the flow of energy around our body, and this will affect our feelings.

Sometimes this links with a part of the body opening or closing, which we have explored, or with increased or decreased tension (as in the seven levels of tension). Often it will also remind us, by association, of situations we have experienced when our bodies felt like this.

These changes can be analysed in terms of a vocabulary of body language which is an inherited instinctive reaction. (At a later stage of exploring body language we find other movements and gestures which are certainly not of this type but are specifically linked to one culture, or even to one small district.)

First, however, we need a sensitivity to look into the different states, and therefore the different stories, which emerge when the body changes from neutral to a particular position, and then from position to position.

To explore this we need a physical control to isolate a single part of the body. As we isolate each part we shall feel the change in our basic body state. In this new state we must be able to explore the space and explore meetings with other people, noting all the time the changes in our feelings, our speed, our rhythm, our reaction-timing.

In such changes we are exploring a new body shape, how it feels, how it plays. It is like putting on a mask and discovering its way of acting and reacting. It will be different from your normal state, but also different for each person doing it.

In this way we build up a sensitivity to the whole body and all its possibilities.

Of particular interest are the changes. When you change between body positions avoid doing it technically. Fix your eyes on a point or a person (it doesn't matter if they don't return the look) and, concentrating on this, slowly go through the change. Be aware how your feelings towards this point or person change. It feels as if they are having an effect on you, whereas in fact you are projecting the story onto them.

Once again we find that although each position is of interest it is often the active phase of changing which is of more interest. Drama thrives on changing.

To effect these changes we work on isolating parts of the body. This needs considerable concentration to allow one part of the body to move without other parts reacting. Such isolation is the basis of a great deal of West African dance-theatre. The exercises of experts such as Peter Badejo and Olu Taiwo use rhythmic isolation to prepare the body for this movement.

With these points as a working base, try the following isolation exercises.

Start with the body neutral:

Exercise 40 Head

A   Push the head forward without changing the rest of the body (see Figure 2.7). In this position feel the difference in yourself, in the way you see the space, and see others. As you start to move allow your walk to be determined by the new balance and new tension in the body. If you are in a new body position your normal walk is bound to change to match this shape. Explore the room and meet other people.[4]

4 With the head in this position the major sense organs are in front of the rest of the body, as they are in almost all other animals. It therefore gives these senses a slightly increased importance. It also places the brain in front and could thus be the position of the 'Thinker', 'Philosopher', etc.

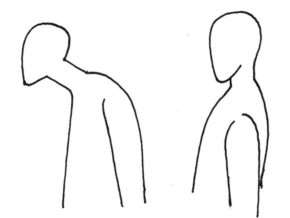

Figure 2.7 Head

5 Here the opposite is true. The senses are behind the line of the body as if you are trying not to see, smell or hear, or as if you are trying to create more distance between you and others (it can often be a position of people in authority who are trying to be impressive: headteachers, policemen, guardsmen, etc.).

It is most important to discover how this position changes you. What are you like in this position? Who are you in this position?

B   Now pull the head right back behind the vertical; feel the change in your body, the new way of moving; explore the space and meet other people.[5]

When you have tried both these positions, explore changing between them, using a stimulus in the room (an object or person) to effect the change. Even with just the head you have a considerable vocabulary. Try a meeting with one partner, only reacting, and therefore speaking, with the head.

Exercise 41 Shoulders

A   From a neutral position pull the shoulders up as high as possible (see Figure 2.8). Explore the changes in feelings, etc. in this position.[6]

B   Push the shoulders right down as far as possible (so far down that they become like a single board across the back) and explore this position. It may only be 1 or 2 centimetres but the difference is palpable.

6 In terms of your body language the shoulders, which are strong, act as shields to protect the weak and vulnerable neck and jugular vein. It can therefore be a protective position, or one of fear. It can also provide the 'armour' of strength to become more aggressive.

Here the shoulders are exposing the neck and jugular, but in such an over-demonstrative way that it is artificially vulnerable. It is as if you are trying to insist 'I am not afraid. I can show my weak parts!'

Play with changing between these two positions while meeting people and finding a stimulus for each change.

C   Now push both shoulders as far forward as possible (see Figure 2.8). Explore the position.

This is another protective position. The shoulders are used to protect the heart/lung zone, and give a nervous, frightened feel. Here the shoulders are good shields but lend little strength to the body.

D   Push both shoulders back as far as possible. Explore the position.

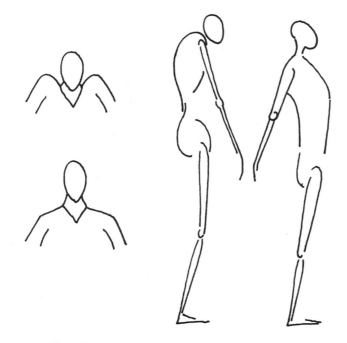

Figure 2.8 Shoulders

This exposes the heart and chest as if nothing could harm you. Again it is an exaggerated position and one interpretation is of over-confidence, over-assuredness.

Change between these two shoulder positions as you move around and meet people. Note what it is like to meet the opposite position to your own. What status changes occur just because one part of the body is isolated and changes position?

Also be aware of the changes in rhythm with each new position and of changes in the spaces you occupy in the room. Do you head for the centre or stick to the walls?

Exercise 42 Chest[7]

It is a very important area and much smaller and more subtle in its movement than the others. Placing the fingers of one hand on the breastbone and allowing them to push the chest back, and be pushed forward by the chest, will help develop this isolation.

7 This is often much more difficult to isolate, especially for European and Asian performers where the spine stays relatively rigid in most movement styles. West African performers, with more variety of spinal movement, find it much easier.

71

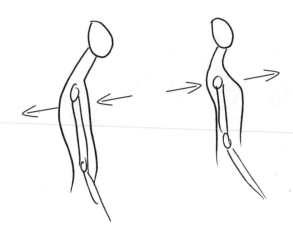

Figure 2.9 Chest

During this movement the shoulders stay absolutely still.

A Push the chest in (backwards) as far as possible (see Figure 2.9). Explore and use this position.

The chest is depressed. The breathing is therefore limited and constricted and not a lot of life-giving air can be converted to energy. It is a position that is sometimes found in mentally depressive patients, and just by taking this position you can again understand the link between physical and psychological states.

Push the chest forward as far as possible and explore the room and other people in this position.

Here there is an openness of the chest and lungs which maximises breathing capacity without any strain. It is by teaching depressed patients to adopt this position that a lot of therapeutic healing has been achieved.

Explore changing between these two, finding your own stimulus to change. Realise that with only a few centimetres of physical change a radical change of mood can be experienced.

Exercise 43 Pelvis

Of course when dealing with this area we are also talking of the genital zone and therefore about sexuality. This can be, and often is, a taboo subject.

This sexuality can of course be blatant – an advanced pelvis could be an 'invitation' and, withdrawn, it could signal fear of sexual contact. However, it can also be a signal which is not directly sexual but a signifier of confidence in one's self.

B Push the pelvis forward, feel the change and explore space and meetings with it leading you (see Figure 2.10).[8]

Pull the pelvis right back and explore space and encounters.

This position almost denies the existence of this area, and pushes the rest of the body forward to compensate and draw attention away from it. This can often be a position of lack of confidence and great nervousness.

Explore both pelvis positions, and the changes between them. As with all changes, experiment with faster and slower movements, forwards, backwards and sideways.

Now try the same exploration on the following positions:

8 There is a particular openness and vulnerability in this position. To walk in it can imply great confidence.

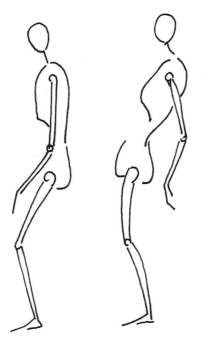

Figure 2.10 Pelvis

- Knees open and closed (see Figure 2.11).

- Walking on the toes – see the world from a few centimetres higher and note how much energy you need to stop.

- Walking on the heels – the weight is thrown back, the body curves to compensate and it is impossible to stand still.

- Walking on the outsides of the feet – this gives a remarkably stable and mobile position (and is like the basic Kathakali position).

- Walking on the insides of the feet – the weight falls inwards and blocks the energy of the lower body.

As the weight changes in these positions so does your balance and therefore your rhythm. These affect your feelings.

When you have been through all these isolations and have felt the effect that the different positions have on your body, it is as if you have learned the various notes on an instrument. Now it is the

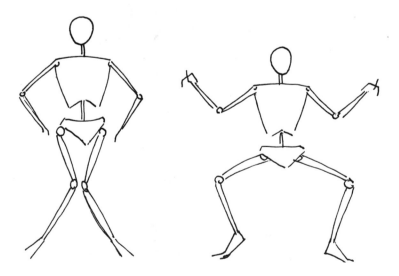

Figure 2.11 Knees open and closed

fluent playing between them that must be achieved. This takes some time but you can start to play with meetings with other people where any part of the body can take the reaction to a stimulus from your partner.

It is a very rich vocabulary through which a vast range of emotions and reactions can be expressed. Sometimes two or more of these body parts can be used to create a character. Sometimes body positions which may be apparently contradictory (e.g. open face and closed pelvis) may be used to show the complexity of a character.

This process also gives you the necessary knowledge to observe and imitate people as a route to finding characters. Looking at people in the street you will now be amazed at how most people show considerable variance from a neutral body. By observing them and analysing body part by body part, you can reconstruct their body with yours and feel what it is like to live in that state.

Moreover there is the possibility of varying the dimensions of each body position from its largest (100 per cent), useful in high emotion or in some stylised forms, to its most subtle (around 5 per cent), useful in very intimate spaces or for camera.

So let us next examine Contradiction and Percentage Dimensions.

CONTRADICTION

It is perhaps one of the basic tenets of all creativity that when you discover something you should also explore its opposite to give depth to your discovery. The next step is for your discovery to contain its opposite.

It is certainly an extremely rich area of research for evolving characters and situations.

All we have studied and developed in this chapter has been to follow an energy-dynamic and to find its natural psychophysical association in a feeling, an emotion, or a character.

But what happens if, having discovered this, we try to work its opposite?

For example, if you are 'open' – your body, arms, face and gestures are all open – we expect a confident, generous character.

If we play the contradiction we can keep this body position but project through it a character which is mean, cruel and nervous.

The message the body gives contradicts the message of, for example, the words, the rhythms, etc. This contradictory message is very interesting as the audience will subconsciously be asking 'why, if he/she seems like this, is he/she acting like that?'

The answer could be that the character is trying to be something other than he/she really is; trying to hide something, trying to convince somebody of something they really do not believe, etc. Or it may be a subconscious side of their character emerging.

It is the world of hypocrisy, of trickery, reflecting a more complex psychology. It is an area which deserves thorough exploration at this stage of training, to acquaint ourselves with all the possibilities and to feel these contradictory forces and what they suggest. It will also be an area to revisit when specifically discovering characters in production to find principal and contradictory forces in them.

Let us look at some of the possibilities of contradictions.

- If you push your head forward from its normal line it will make you want to follow it and move forward, as it is an inquisitive position and is throwing the body-weight forward. Try this position now, only moving backward.

  It will feel strange but try to find out who you are and what are the psychological contradictions which emerge from doing it.

- Try to use only very geometric gestures but (the contradiction) speak tenderly to a lover.

- Work in level 6 of tension (see the seven levels of tension) and speak about how relaxed you are.

- Push the shoulders forward (defensive position) and attack somebody, verbally, then physically.

Try all of these, look at the contradictory feelings and try to understand the story of why this person behaves in this contradictory way.

Characters become richer, multi-layered, more unexpected and surprising.

I am always reminded of a fascinating phenomenon in nature. There is a particular toad which is hunted by snakes. When confronted by the snake, you would think it would try to make itself small, unnoticeable, camouflaged, so that it could escape quickly.

This toad does the opposite. Although in mortal danger, it gulps in air to bloat itself to double its normal size and then very slowly retreats. Presumably its 'defence' is based on confusing the snake, or presenting itself as too awesome or too big to eat. It is the contradiction of its situation.

PERCENTAGE DIMENSIONS (EXPANSION AND CONTRACTION)

We often talk of 'stylised theatre'. In Europe this invariably means non-naturalistic or non-realistic theatre and refers to heightened speech or movement.

In fact naturalism and realism are also styles and therefore 'stylised'. Unfortunately 'stylised theatre' is often considered to be less credible. Of course credibility has nothing to do with the style of theatre, it has to do with the truth of the situation (after all, Shakespeare is highly stylised speech but we readily believe in the characters and situations).

All that we do on stage is stylised but the level of stylisation differs. As we move from the small intimate naturalist plays in studio theatres to the broad dance-drama styles with extreme make-up and movement in front of thousands (e.g. in south and south-east Asia, but also Greek tragedy), it is the dimension of playing which changes.

It is as if the internal dynamic and motivation (thus the honesty) of the playing is constant but if played at 10 per cent of the body's most extreme scale it could be labelled naturalism; at 30–40 per cent it may be used for comedy, farce, musical comedy; at 60–70 per cent we are in the area of epic drama, tragedy, and above this we enter the world of Kathakali, Noh, Beijing Opera, Topeng and melodrama.

We can easily explore this idea:

Try to make a single large gesture, as large as you can, with the whole hand, arm, body and balance engaged totally. This is your 100 per cent. Do it many times until you really feel the full movement and the feeling it inspires.

Now keep exactly the same physical impulses in the body but only allow the movement to cover 75 per cent of its potential. Only the dimensions changes, not the internal dynamic of it.

Now allow it to cover only 50 per cent of its potential.

Now 25 per cent. This is probably the type of gesture used in a modern European play, based on realism.

Now try 10 per cent. The feeling is the same, but the movement is very small. This could be used for a TV or film close-up.

Now 5 per cent. You can feel it but it would be quite difficult for anyone else to see it.

Now 1 per cent. This is virtually invisible although all the muscles involved in the first movement are still engaged.

As the movement is concentrated to this 'kernel' of its possibility, you may have different associations connected to it. This is because we use different levels in different situations in our lives, but the dynamic and honesty of the movement stay the same.

This is an excellent way to examine any movement. By playing it on different levels you can see where it strikes chords in you.

9 Elsa Wolliaston uses exactly this technique to explore and understand the physical language of African dance-theatre. She starts with a small gesture pattern, e.g. sewing with needle and thread, or cutting with a knife, and slowly expands this to its maximum. She can then play the 'scale' from 0–100 per cent of this movement.

Try the opposite. A small everyday movement (probably already at about 10 per cent). Expand it to 20 per cent, 50 per cent, 75 per cent and 100 per cent. You may be amazed at the new meanings the movement takes on as it covers more space.

But remember it is always the same movement and does not become more or less 'right' as it changes dimensions.[9]

ELEMENT IDENTIFICATION

EMOTIONAL AND CHARACTER ASSOCIATION WITH THE ELEMENTS FIRE, WATER, AIR, EARTH

This is the beginning of a fascinating series of association exercises by which you can channel your energies in a more complex way to discover different rhythms, tensions and flows in the body. These in turn lead you towards characters who are identifiable with the elements, and later steel, glass, rubber, then colours, animals, etc.

It is a way of discovering and constructing a character which relies on imaginative identification, rather than a psychological construction. This does not mean it cannot be used in conjunction with a psychological approach, but it often does not need it.

Exercise 44 Element identification

Visualisation

Close the eyes. Deepen the breathing. In your mind visualise fire in front of you. It can be any sort of fire, but it is easier to start with quite a large fire; a bonfire or even a forest fire. Hold that image in your mind. Let your breathing become the breathing of the fire you are visualising. It is important that this is not the breathing of you burning in fire but the shape, form and rhythm of fire itself; the hot burning centre and the flames leaping up and up with no corresponding downward movement.

Into the movement

Slowly allow the rhythm you have found in the breathing to enter the whole body. The torso will already be moving with the breath. Allow the neck, head, arms and legs also to move with it, so your whole body takes on the rhythm of fire. Open your eyes and start to move in the space with it. Notice how you travel, how you cover the space and react to the room.

Bringing it towards character

Continuing the full movement, start to meet others in the space. Notice how you meet, how your movements coincide, clash, inspire other movements, repel or attract. The movement at this point is extended and still abstract but is now becoming reactive to others. It has types of meetings, a distinct way of reacting.

Maintaining the element in character

Keep the full breathing, rhythm and movement in your body but now concentrate this into 50 per cent of its fullest range. Continue meeting and relating your element-rhythm to the space and to the other people. The movement is no longer so far beyond the range of everyday expression. Now you are maintaining the fire as your essence, your driving force, but also becoming a human with an existence shaped by this element.

Then reduce it to 25 per cent. At this level you are within normal human expressive range. Notice the kind of gestural language which develops for your character. Then reduce to 10 per cent.

By this time your body language is back within an everyday social range of human movement but every reaction is in the language of your element. You have developed a 'fire character' at quite a naturalistic level. Try it in different situations.

By repeating the above process with water, air and earth, other types of characters appear.

For water, concentrate on the flow and the weight. It virtually never stops. It flows around things and always falls heavily downwards if it rises.

For air, concentrate again on its flow, but air can come to a stopped suspension and has no weight, no reliance on gravity. It can move up or down or sideways depending on its force and the obstacles it meets in its path.

For earth, think of the clay that is used in sculpture or pottery. If you push it, it gives way to your push and stays there. There is no rebound, only a heavy acceptance of moulding, indentation, etc.

Having followed this process you are able to identify an element and then find the energy of this identification in a character.

You can then set up simple scenes of meetings of such characters. How do they meet to confront, to flirt? How do they wait in a doctor's waiting room?

Now try to use the same process with other elements. Try to identify with oil, with paper, with glass and then onwards to spaghetti (cooked!), steam, even toothpaste. They will all lead you to a different use of your energy, to a different character.

3   The energy of rhythm

As we become exposed to, and interested in, world theatre forms we become rapidly aware of the intimate relationship of action, text and music. Although there are music-theatre forms in European culture with their own histories and traditions, the majority of Western theatre exists without these layers of emotional, evocative and commentating expression.

The relationships of the music to performer are varied, complex and often culturally specific. But contained within each is an element which can be enormously helpful to any performer: the element of *rhythm*.

Even here there are varying forms and relationships of rhythm in performance but there is a dynamic in rhythm which can make a performer more precise, more in time with other performers, more linked to the audience on a common pulse, in short, more expressive.

Whether it is the use of complex rhythms in Kathakali, where rhythms are suited to particular moods, the Beijing Opera actor's ability to work on a rhythm and then break it to keep the audience always alert and surprised, or the Yoruba bata tradition of performers signalled into new actions by changes of rhythm, we are in a world of being excited and inspired by the relationship with the pulse.

Physical Theatre has long realised the value of rhythm. Dario Fo works his scenes by vocalising the rhythm of an entry, a look, an exchange, just as any Bharata Natyam dancer might, and clowns can rehearse scenes beat by beat. But all too often we ignore the training of rhythm and rely on the slightly ephemeral quality of 'timing'.

The problem with 'timing' is that we tend to think an actor either has it or does not. It is given some mystical quality, rather than being an object of learning, training and mastery.

By looking at the way in which rhythm is organised, learned and used in different performance styles we can develop an inner pulse and a division of that pulse to open a new vocabulary for ourselves. With this new sensitisation to rhythm 'timing' doesn't seem so difficult.

But first a quick word for those performers who have a dread of rhythm. Often this is because it has been associated with music, which is seen as an 'other' art form than theatre. It is an unfounded fear. Just walk around a room or along a street. Inevitably you will fall into a regular beat. You have set up a pulse, the prerequisite of rhythmic work.

Or listen to music and notice how your foot taps in time with it. Or take part in any form of social dancing, on any type of dance floor and your feet, arms, spine are all synchronised to the rhythm. We all have this capacity. We just have to accept it, examine it and use it.

Rhythm is the division of silence and stillness into organised and repeatable units, whether it is the 'one, two' of walking or the intricacies of Zambian Nyau mask play.

So here is how we can start …

A useful definition of rhythm for us could be that of Sivasankaram Pannikar, who calls it 'Energy placed in time and space in units which make us come alive'.

Or perhaps that of Elsa Wolliaston: 'silence divided by patterns of our expression'.

These both remind us that the base of rhythm is not its complexity but its simple root in energy and stillness. And directly stemming from this is the fact that listening and waiting is the key to starting work in rhythm.

We need to listen; we need to establish a basic beat, a pulse that we can keep. This becomes our energy base which we can then vary and measure.

This chapter will cover:

- Finding a pulse
- Keeping the pulse
- Dividing the pulse

- Rhythm in the body
- Asymmetric rhythm
- Speech on the rhythm
- Character through rhythm.

FINDING A PULSE

To get going here is a rhythm game which eases us into this exciting world.

Exercise 45 Names and visual co-ordination

This is a wonderful game to break the ice at the beginning of a training session or rehearsal, but demands great concentration to transfer visual signals into rhythm.

It should be set up quite slowly – make sure that each phase is running smoothly before the next one is introduced.

Phase 1

The group stands in a circle. Everybody claps on a 3 beat:

1	2	3
CLAP	CLAP	OPEN (i.e. no clap)

One by one, go around the circle, each person inserting his or her name into the open space.

1	2	3
CLAP	CLAP	NAME

Go once around the circle (remember, everybody claps all the time, only one speaks at a time).

Phase 2

Now you must pick one visible distinguishing feature which some of the group have (e.g. those wearing white trousers). Ideally in a group of 12, 3 or 4 should have this distinguishing feature.

The clapping continues around the circle as in phase 1 (clap-clap-name). When the name-saying comes to a person with the new visual signal, everybody does:

1	2	**3**	4
CLAP	CLAP	**STAMP**	NAME
		(RIGHT FOOT)	

This is on the same rhythmic pulse (so the first was a 3 beat and this is a 4 beat).

As you go around the names you will thus be changing between:

CLAP   CLAP   NAME

and

CLAP   CLAP   STAMP   NAME

Work at it until it is smooth and everyone is clapping and stamping in unison.

Phase 3

Find one more distinctive feature (e.g. red T-shirts). It is all right if only 1 or 2 people have these.

When you reach the time for these people to say their names everybody does:

1	2	3	**4**	5
CLAP	CLAP	STAMP	**CLAP**	NAME

(This is a 5 beat phrase.)

Phase 4

Choose one more visual feature (e.g. striped clothes), and when these people are reached the sequence is:

1	2	3	4	**5**	6
CLAP	CLAP	STAMP	CLAP	**STAMP**	NAME

(This is a 6 beat phrase.)

Phase 5

If you can find one more feature (it may be only one person, e.g. with a beard, with a headscarf, etc.), the sequence is:

1	2	3	4	5	**6**	7
CLAP	CLAP	STAMP	CLAP	STAMP	**CLAP**	NAME
					BEHIND BACK	

(This is a 7 beat phrase.)[1]

1 If someone has more than one of the chosen visual signals the later one overrides the earlier.

When you reach this stage just seeing a visual signal is the trigger to change rhythm and you are constantly changing between a 3, 4, 5, 6 and 7 beat phrase. Although it may have taken some time to develop this exercise it is not difficult for a group to be quite fluent in this sequence after 15 minutes.

By following this everyone has been introduced to:

- holding a pulse as a group
- varying easily between phrases of 3 to 7 beats
- watching for signals to change rhythms
- not counting a rhythm.

This last 'not counting a rhythm' is very important. The rhythms are introduced and learned as physical patterns of action not as counted patterns in the head. If we can achieve this it becomes much easier to work with rhythm without getting into mathematical tangles in our minds.

The exercise can go further. Here are some possibilities:

Change positions

If you have been standing in a circle for the whole development of the exercise you will have established a constantly repeating pattern. This pattern can become the way of remembering the rhythms, rather than watching and reacting.

So change positions in the circle. You are now next to a different person with different distinguishing signals.

Play through phase 5 again, and a new pattern emerges.

Silence as a beat

Play the game exactly as before (phase 5), but instead of speaking your name, keep silent. You must still mark the same space as if your name were being spoken. The silence becomes an 'audible' part of the rhythm pattern.

You need extra alertness to follow the pattern around the circle as you no longer have the names as markers, but you can also start to hear the changing and interlocking patterns of rhythms and appreciate their beauty.[2]

2 If someone had asked you to divide up 3 beat, 4 beat, 5 beat, 6 beat and 7 beat phrases amongst the group it would have become an intensely difficult mental exercise. You have entered a game with rhythm through another, physicalised route. Just as we don't count when dancing socially in a nightclub, we have found a 'felt' route to patterns.

KEEPING THE PULSE

In the last exercise we were playing in and around a strong pulse but these exercises concentrate more precisely on holding an inner pulse, and on keeping a pulse in a group.

Exercise 46 Passing and feeling the pulse

You stand in a circle, close enough to touch your neighbour's shoulder. One person claps four regularly spaced claps. By listening to these four claps the pulse is set up. You continue it by making an audible action on the pulse:

The first person raises his/her right hand and places it on the next person's shoulder with a slight audible slap on the beat. Leave the hand there. That person raises their hand and places it on the next person's shoulder on the next beat of the pulse, and so on. The pulse is kept going, and heard, by the placing of hands on shoulders all around the group.

Until … all right hands are up on the neighbours' shoulders. Continue the sounding of the pulse one by one, but this time let the hand descend from the shoulder and gently hit your thigh on the beat, and the next, and the next, until you are all back at your starting positions.

You will become quickly aware that it is more difficult to keep the pulse from accelerating when the hand is descending from shoulder to thigh. Gravity is accelerating it, and care has to be taken to find the muscular control to keep on the pulse.

Play this through several times. Each time you start try to change the pulse. In general you will find that faster pulses are easier to keep than slower ones.

In fulfilling this exercise you have started to feel rhythm in operation, actions meeting the exact point of a pulse.

A further development demands even greater control.

Exercise 47 Jump on it

One person claps a relatively slow four regular beats to establish the basic pulse.

The person on his/her right jumps *to land on the beat*, the next jumps to land on the next beat and so on around the circle.

All jumps are slightly different, depending on the individual, so the vital point is to land correctly. For higher jumps you may have to take off slightly earlier or for small jumps the take-off can be left later, but the landing, and the sound of the landing, maintains the steady pulse.

Exercise 48 The running clap

This is an excellent game for rhythmic training, and for learning to co-ordinate as an indispensable member of a group.

Stand in a circle, with a double arm's length between you.

A clap is to be 'passed' around the circle, from right to left.

The first person stretches towards the person to the left, makes eye contact and claps towards him or her. This person accepts the gesture as if gathering it between the hands, takes it in towards the body, then through to the left, stretching towards the next person, and claps to the next person.

In this way it travels right around the circle. Very important is the sense of taking the clap from the last person and giving it to the next one.

The rhythm of the game is determined entirely by the second person to clap. The timing between the first clap and the second clap sets the pulse so the third person must clap with exactly the same interval.

Thus the rhythm is established.

There is always a tendency with rhythm-based exercises for the rhythm to speed up. Be very careful not to let the rhythm run away. Try to hear exactly the pulse as set up by the first and second people, and hold it between each clap as it goes around the circle.

As soon as someone is in front or behind the beat, stop and start again. You can easily work for 15 or 20 minutes each day on this to get absolute precision and co-ordination.

Extension

When the clap is well under control, after 10 to 12 circles, you can allow an extremely slow and even acceleration to take place. It should be imperceptible; no one person should try to speed it up. Extreme concentration is needed so that it does not slow down again nor run away too fast.

After many circuits the clap will be running around the circle very fast like an electric spark along a wire, as if the energy of the group is released. It is a very exciting ending to the game.

We have the pulse; we are feeling it not as a counted piece of mathematics but as a body-mind continuum. The more we can internalise the pulse, the more we can use the rhythm as a foundation to help the clarity and precision of our play.

Exercise 49 Dividing the pulse

Clapping together on a fairly fast beat is not too challenging. The tension inherent in a rhythm becomes apparent as we start to hear the silence between beats and anticipate the coming beat, whether as a clap, a foot-beat, a word, a move or a gesture.

For this we simply divide the beat.

Start with a regular clapping (line 1 in Figure 3.1). When this is established we start to leave out every second clap (line 2).

This becomes the new clapping rhythm. Make sure it is steady, then leave out every second beat from this pulse (line 3). Establish this as a steady beat. Again 'halve it' by leaving out every second beat (line 4). Consolidate it and again halve it (line 5).

This seems relatively simple and indeed it would be if we were all counting aloud.

But without counting aloud we are holding the pulse inside us and stretching the tension between beats until at line 5 there is an enormous sense of anticipation of the beat, and resolution of that pregnancy when the beat is reached.

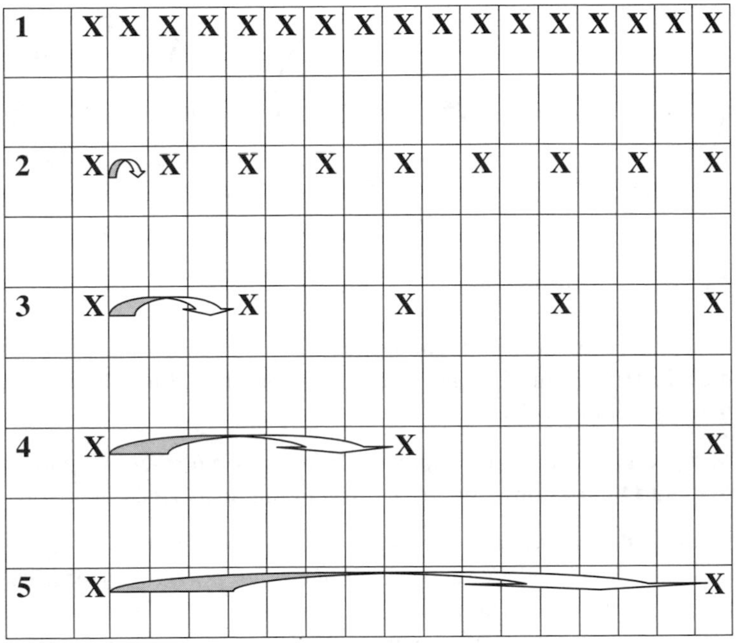

1	X	X	X	X	X	X	X	X	X	X	X	X	X	X	X	X
2	X		X		X		X		X		X		X		X	
3	X			X				X				X				X
4	X						X									X
5	X															X

Figure 3.1 Dividing the pulse

How do we hold the pulse?

When we first do this exercise many people visualise the rhythm by tapping the foot, bobbing the head, beating the hand in the air or using other personal devices. They are 'conducting' the beat externally.

This may be acceptable for a musician but of course it would be very distracting for an actor. Whilst rhythm may come to a performer through audible percussion, we also need to be able to use it without an external pulse.

Similarly many people continue to count 'in their heads' to keep the beat. In the above clapping exercise that would be counting to 2, 4, 8, 16, etc. But such counting fills the head with arithmetic and will be difficult to hold onto if we are also using text, holding a dialogue, contacting emotions, etc. We need to internalise it differently.

This may take several attempts, but we can be helped by certain images.

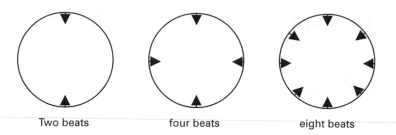

| Two beats | four beats | eight beats |

Figure 3.2 Rhythm visualisation

Many north Indian (Hindustani) musicians visualise the rhythm as a circle broken into pulses at regular intervals, rather like a clock face (see Figure 3.2).

Many west African performers inwardly 'sing' a non-verbal pattern to fit into the rhythm, and let that roll in the head whilst working.

Practise the above division and sub-division until you are not counting aloud, not counting in your head, and not making the pulse visible anywhere in the body. This may take a little time and you will have to find the device which best suits you to achieve this.

RHYTHM IN THE BODY

Exercise 50 From hands to feet to gestures to eyes

This is exactly the same exercise but the beats are marked with the feet. As soon as this becomes easy you can move around the stage. With this mobility meetings are possible, reactions are easier, based on the rhythm.

Start in a circle, with the group setting up a regular step, just audible and not too fast, from left foot to right to left, etc. on the spot.

Then with every step add a simple gesture, pointing, beckoning, halting, etc. which ends precisely on the pulse.

And with every gesture let the eyes go with the gesture and meet their focus on the pulse.

So you have a very precise set of movements clearly on the beat.

Then halve the beat. As you then step and gesture only on every second beat, you are fixed in strong, directed, decided positions from which you can slowly withdraw to prepare for the next beat. As the beats are halved further and further, this withdrawing can travel further, observing the space and other people, and preparing for where the next beat will come.

Once you are able to carry out this exercise fluently you will notice how defined your movements and positions have become by using the rhythm.

Such clarity can be very useful in setting up Image Theatre exercises.

Holding your own

A useful development of the above exercise is to work through it slowly but leave 2 or 3 members of the group at each stage. As a result you will finish with small groups on different divisions of the pulse (lines 1 to 5 in Figure 3.1). Let them move through the space, meeting each other, holding on to their own division of rhythm whilst interacting with others. The mood and character change with each division from fast and light to slow and strong, and the meetings bring out some of the potential of rhythm for mood and character development.

The silent rhythm

Now try to repeat the above exercise with this addition. Once all the groups are established, take away the percussive foot-beat which has been marking the rhythm division. You are left marking the rhythm with strong accurate gestures and eye movements. It has an uncanny feel. The group is bonded by an unheard force; it is very focused, very accurate. We, the viewers, know that something is bonding these actions, but we know not what. Such communication through rhythm is excellent for chorus work.

Exercise 51 Apply it

Rhythm can be used to express change of mood, to clarify and project relationships and to give a clear and viewable body. After the journey through the rhythm exercises above you can now really play with it.

Stand in a circle. Everyone sets up a light stamping pulse. One person enters the circle walking on that pulse. With every look at someone else in the circle, change your rhythm. You can use the above changes, halving again and again, doubling it (adding two beats for every one), or stress the 'off-beat' (the beat between the main beats of the pulse – it has a very dynamic tension). Alternatively, if you are confident playing with the rhythm you can react to someone with a more complex pattern, but still linked to the group's pulse.

Keep each new rhythm going as you face that person; use it to approach them, or retreat from them. As you turn to see another person change the rhythm again. Try this with 3 or 4 people, and then return to the circle.

The next person enters, and so on until everyone has experienced rhythm as a means of reacting.

We are touching something very basic here. We all realise that in moments of excitement we move to a faster, crisper rhythm, in moments of shock the rhythm changes again. Every day we experience hundreds of changes of rhythm when our thoughts change, when impulses around us change.

This exercise allows us to externalise and heighten this internal rhythmic score.

Remember … rhythm is not just in the stamp of the foot – although that is a very good place to start. Gestures, turns of the head, changes of position are all ways of marking the rhythm.

Remember … that silence and stillness are important parts of rhythm. You don't have to be moving constantly. By waiting, watching and re-starting on the beat you build up one of the most important dramatic elements of rhythm: anticipation.

Exercise 52 Rhythm conversations

During that last exercise many people in the circle feel the need to respond to the performer in the middle. This exercise draws on that.

Start again from the circle and a regular foot stamping rhythm. One person enters the circle on the beat, changes the rhythm on facing someone else, and then that person answers the new rhythm and uses it to move into the circle.

Then the conversation commences. One offers a rhythm with feet, body and gesture. The second answers it, just as in a spoken conversation, and each offering is answered by the next. Occasionally they may overlap, and occasionally there may be silences – conversations are like that. The important thing is that a progressive communication is established using the rhythmic body as the 'voice'.

ASYMMETRIC RHYTHMS

In European cultures the vast majority of rhythm is based on a 4 beat phrase. It is also widely used in folk theatre and folk dance in most parts of the world. It seems to be the easiest to move to, and to build phrases with. European cultures also use a 2 beat (the march) and a 3 beat (the waltz) but very little which is more complex than that, except in avant-garde music.

Many other world theatre traditions use more complex rhythms to great effect. Rhythms of 5 or 7 beat phrases are only the beginning of this, but they can reveal very strong dynamics which can help our performance.

Drawing from the Indian rhythm systems in music we find a way of understanding these more complex rhythms and of building and using them.

The following is an adaptation of a very complex system which can be studied for many years with its teachers. These are very simple building blocks of rhythm. I have simplified the consonants which can be learned as follows:

Clapping a simple pulse divide them into

- A 2 beat: *Ta* ka *Ta* ka *Ta* ka
- A 3 beat: *Ta* ki ta *Ta* ki ta
- A 4 beat: *Ta* ka di mi *Ta* ka di mi

Clap a stronger beat on the *Ta* which starts each cycle and clap lighter beats for the others.

To build more complex rhythms, simply build these units together.

So for example a 5 beat becomes:

Ta ka <u>plus</u> *Ta* ki ta = *Ta* ka *ta* ki ta

which has the strongest clap on the first *Ta* and a relatively strong beat on the second *ta*. This central beat gives the driving force of the asymmetric structure.[3]

3 For our purposes we could reverse the order to be *Ta* ki ta *ta* ka.

A 7 beat cycle becomes:

Ta ki ta <u>plus</u> *Ta* ka di mi = *Ta* ki ta *ta* ka di mi

Again with one strong beat on the first *Ta*, a secondary beat on the middle *ta* and the rest light beats. Clap this until you feel that driving force of the two unequal parts of this rhythmic unit.[4]

When we progress to a 9 beat phrase we use all three of our building block units as:

Ta ka *ta* ki ta *ta* ka di mi

Try it!

If you achieve this, you can progress to build more complex rhythm structures, of eleven, thirteen, fifteen, with relative ease. This is excellent for increasing rhythmic awareness but you are unlikely to use such structures even in highly stylised work.

4 Again we could reverse the order to be *Ta* ka di mi *ta* ki ta.

Exercise 53 Feeling through the feet

Set up a regular rhythm in the feet from left foot to right foot with no specific accent.

Then follow the above progress by accenting the three base building blocks with a strong foot-beat on the first *ta* of each one.

Notice here that on the 'even number' beats (2 and 4) you will always start the phrase with an accent on the same foot, with the 'odd number' 3 beat you start alternate phrases on the opposite foot.

As you build a 5 beat (ta ka ta ki ta) or a 7 beat (ta ki ta ta ka di mi), these, being odd numbers, also start on a different foot with each phrase. In this way the asymmetric structure of the rhythm becomes physically apparent.

Add hand gestures and eye directions and your whole body is engaged in these complex structures in a surprisingly simple way.

Once internalised you can use these rhythms to travel, to meet, and to react. Start with:

Exercise 54 Crossing the circle

1   *Ta ki ta*. Let the whole group, in a circle, mark the rhythm with the feet. One by one cross the circle adding gestures and eye focus. When everyone has crossed repeat it but not stressing every single beat. Rather, use the ta ki ta as a foundation for pauses, starts and stops. The rhythm can be marked with a turn of the body, a gesture, a change of eye direction. The possibilities are endless. But notice how the 3 beat gives you a different feeling to a 2 beat or 4 beat.

2   *Ta ka Ta ki ta*. Repeat the above process on this 5 beat but be aware of the internal structure by stressing both the *ta* sounds – *ta* ka *ta* ki ta – and feel how it drives you across the circle.

3   *Ta ki ta Ta ka di mi*. Again repeat the process, and again be aware of the internal beats *ta* ki ta *ta* ka di mi. Mark them with foot-beats, gestures, turns, drops to the floor or stillness.

Soon you will be able to use the rhythms as a base on which you can build gestures, movements and vocal sounds with extreme precision and confidence.

It can help for a leader to provide a gentle reminder of the through-going pulse with claves or hand-drum. This can be withdrawn as the participants build up their comfort with the pulse and rhythm structure.

ACTIONS WITH EVERYDAY OBJECTS

Until now we have been working mainly on the technique of understanding and executing rhythmic phrases, while noting how it clarifies our expression. In highly stylised production work we may perform with this clearly stated rhythmic pattern, but more often the rhythm is a base on which we build our performance.

If the rhythm is held throughout sequences of speech or movement, either externally (an instrument) or internally (holding it yourself, or through the rhythm of the speech), it provides a common pulse to link performer and audience.

With the rhythm established we can place words or actions, silences or physical stops within that rhythm, to maximise their effect.

To exercise this set up a simple scene. In the space, place a table, two chairs and some objects on the table: a cup, newspaper, etc.

Establish a rhythm externally with claves, hand clap or small drum. Start with a simple pattern of four.

Enter the space. Move around the space feeling the rhythm in the way you move, look and react to the space. Then feel it in your decisions – the moments of going to a chair, lifting the cup, etc.

You do not have to move on every beat, not even on the first, strong, beat of each phrase. Rather you should use the rhythm's pulse for when you want to act or react. Let it help you extend pauses, accentuate moments, etc. When you have tried it a few times the enormous possibilities of doing this will become apparent.

Each interaction with the space needs only last 1 or 2 minutes. Soon it will become not just easy, but the clarity of play with rhythm will allow you to manipulate the space and the rhythm and discover strengths within it.

Now try the same exercise on a 5 beat, then a 7 beat, then a 9 beat. Notice how the mood changes with the change of rhythm structure.

Now try each of the above situations with two people in the space. Here you are working with the rhythm as a support but also being inspired by the actions of the other person. Soon you will realise how linked the two of you are by the pulse. One of the strengths of rhythm in performance is that the audience not only sees the bond of the performers but feels part of that bond as they are also feeling the pulse.

It will take a number of attempts to feel free with the above exploration. When you have achieved this, move to the next stage.

This is to repeat all of the explorations of space and rhythm *without* the external rhythm. Now you are holding the pulse internally. Try not to count it, but to hold the structure of it in the whole of your being, not just your thoughts.

With this achieved you have made enormous progress and have entered the world of:

TIMING THROUGH RHYTHM

When Dario Fo thinks through a scene to a vocalised rhythm, or a Chhau performer prepares to go onstage, repeating the rhythms of the performance, or a clown or comedian runs through 'à l'italien', i.e. without fully performing, just marking the movements with tiny gestures, they are all checking the timing of their work by checking the rhythm.

The rhythm is in your control, to lengthen or speed up the moves, actions, gestures or words, but being able to control it is the essence of timing.

William Chow, a Beijing Opera actor now teaching in the USA, talks of the importance in his form of setting up a rhythm and then surprising the audience by breaking it. This use of rhythmic expectation to keep an audience's attention has great theatrical possibilities.

Try a very simple phrase of actions, e.g. a walk, turn, point and step back. Now try to recapture it by vocalising the exact rhythm of what you just did. Use any sound which seems appropriate to capture the dynamics of what you have done.

If you are not happy with the result try changing the vocalised rhythm then executing the action sequence on that. By moving between one and the other you soon become very conscious of the timing needed to optimise your work.

This is not the heavily structured rhythm of the divisions of 4, 5 or 9, but it creates a rhythm to underline and support what you are doing.

SPEECH ON THE RHYTHM

From the extended speech patterns of Noh Theatre to the Dub performances of the Caribbean, from the theatrical story-telling of India's Pandavani to the use of rap in anti-drugs and anti-violence theatre for development projects, speech to rhythm has all the drive and precision that we have seen in movement and gesture. European theatre of course has a similarly long tradition of rhythmic speech, from Shakespeare to Eliot, Euripides to Yeats, although the rhythm is now often sacrificed to achieve more psychologically 'real' phrasing.

The heightening of speech through rhythm brings a dynamism to it which is immensely attractive.

One route to achieving this is by studying given texts to discover their rhythm; another is to take a prose text and give it a rhythmic framework. Both of these, however, need a familiarity with the playfulness rhythm can provide.

A good exercise to ease into this is as follows:

Sit in a circle. Keep a steady pulse in the group, clapping lightly or with a small drum.

One by one start to describe something very simple on the beat:

- Describe what you had for breakfast
- Describe your journey to work/the workshop/class
- Describe what you are wearing.

The only thing to avoid is speaking one syllable to one beat, which becomes very monotonous (or, rather, mono-rhythmic). On the contrary you can stretch a syllable over several beats, then two syllables to a beat, wait several beats before speaking, or repeat a phrase on the beat before continuing.

Very quickly the rhythm serves as a base to stretch and play with the words and the ability to communicate and emphasise what you are saying.

Even at this stage a simple addition takes you to a very common theatrical story-telling structure:

The group decides on a question to launch the above descriptions, and decides on a rhythmic structure for it, e.g. 'Tell us how you got here today'.

The group speaks this in unison on the agreed beat (e.g. over 4 beats) as a 'group call' to elicit the 'response' (e.g. over 8 beats) as above from an individual. The exercise continues with:

Group call
Individual response
Group call
Individual response
Etc.

This call and response structure is found in proto-theatrical narrative forms all over the world.

CHARACTER THROUGH RHYTHM

It is clear to us that every character we ever develop on stage has a different body shape, a different psychological shape, a different balance of weight. All these give each character a different basic rhythm. From this rhythm they may speed up, slow down, syncopate, etc. as they meet different situations and emotions but there is still a baseline rhythm which is different from your own.

Finding this baseline rhythm can be a very useful window to a character, and yet we rarely explore it.

To experience this possibility is not difficult if you have succeeded in internalising rhythms, as above.

Exercise 55 Character – rhythms

Work in twos. One person creates a rhythmic phrase. This can be clapped or vocalised. It can be as long or as short as you like. This will be the base for finding a character. Rather obviously long slow regular rhythms will lead to very different characters than rapid, asymmetric, changing rhythms.

When your rhythm is clear and you can vocalise it in any way you want, teach it to your partner. They will:

- First vocalise it with you

- Then vocalise it alone

- Then vocalise it while moving and allowing the rhythm to create a physical pattern of steps, turns, reactions, timings, etc.

- Then internalise the rhythm so it is not sounded but held in the body movements.

As they move with the rhythm they allow that physical pattern to become their way of being, their way of reacting and their way of meeting. It is not that the movements are identical with each repetition of the rhythmic phrase, but the rhythm which underlies the changing movement is a constant. The physical rhythm and its experiences thus suggest a psychology. When you are moving to this rhythm it is not you as you normally are. It is a different persona you are sketching. It is, in fact, a different character.

If you are doing this in a group, half of you (those who created the rhythms) will be watching the other half who have created these differing personas. Notice how those people have changed in their physical appearance and in their emotional appearance, due to the rhythm base you have given. Notice how different they all are from each other!

Allow them to meet: there is a world of emergent characters starting to interact.

Extension 1

As you repeat this exercise don't just create a random rhythm to pass on to your partner, create one with a particular intention of character. Try to create, for example, a mercurial character or a pedantic or a depressive or an impulsive character.

Watch your partner take it on and see how close the resulting character is to your intention.

Extension 2

Think of a character from an existing play, or a character you are working to create. Working from an idea of that character's psychology or from the text and the type of phrases of his/her dialogue, create a rhythmic phrase which suggests that character's inner impulses. Start to move on that rhythmic phrase. Your steps, your weight shifts, your eye movements, even your breathing will use it as a base.

The rhythm gives you a way of physicalising the character and bringing your internal understanding to an external expression.

This is a rich area for further research in your personal quest for characters as a performer. You can also watch people in the street and try to track their movement on a rhythmic phrase. Don't worry if it is not 100 per cent consistent: onstage we are heightening what we see in life, and anyway there will always be inconsistencies and breaks in the rhythm. These are the unexpected moments which bring life and credibility to the drama of a character.

4 Improvisation

The actor does not go on stage to make something happen, but to let something happen.

- Defining improvisation
- Improvisation – the first steps
- Solo improvisations
- Improvisations with two people
- Improvisation with variation of absolutes
- A group improvisation.

DEFINING IMPROVISATION

Improvisation is the key to creativity. Improvisation is one of the actor's most important ways of bringing new moments, situations and atmospheres into play.

Yet just the word 'improvisation' strikes fear into the hearts of so many actors. It is because the word is used too generally, meaning too many things. It is also because the actor is usually not trained to explore improvisation step by step as a fascinating path of discovery. Rather he or she is asked to face the unknown with insufficient 'tools' and therefore feels very vulnerable. Virtually everything you have been doing in this book has been such an exploration. You have, by following the given suggestions, prompts and frameworks, been improvising.

So let us try to clear the 'fog' of confusion surrounding improvisation and try to identify what it is and find a path through it.

Many may think of improvisation as a very Western, contemporary phenomenon. Certainly it has been a key word and method for the avant-garde of experimental theatre and dance, useful for finding new approaches to performance, especially work which is not primarily text-based.

But improvisation exists in many forms and in many performance traditions. By considering these for a moment we may achieve a better view of the whole area of work. We shall also become aware that although we are looking for something new and appropriate in each improvisation we can only work with what we have.

So a Noh Theatre actor, in that wonderful form which seems so fixed and classical to Western trained performers, in fact has considerable flexibility in just how a piece is performed at any one time. It is a tradition for a Noh actor to stand for a while before the performance and listen to the audience to gauge whether they are relaxed, tired, excitable, etc. and to modify the performance accordingly. How is this done? By using his own vocabulary, the Noh form, but varying that form subtly. He can use more or less speed, more or less repetition of phrases by signalling his intentions to the musicians, and more force in his gestures. These are small variations, but variation is the beginning of improvisation. Most importantly he is reacting and changing to the needs of the moment to find something new for that audience.

In performances of Kathakali in south India this variation has rather more space to develop. Again the form is, to a large degree, a set form but individual actors, and especially individual characters, have considerable freedom within the form. I have seen a Kathakali performance in a Kerala village, where the actor playing Hanuman, the monkey god, exercised considerable freedom. When he entered the playing area the local children sitting at the front of the audience greeted him with glee (Hanuman is always a popular character). He responded by leaving his 'set' movement score and played threatening them unless they kept quiet, pleading with them to sit still. He was down on his knees, he found a chair and pretended running at them with it and much more. It was entirely 'in the moment' almost like a Lecoq clown exercise. But at no moment did he leave his Kathakali vocabulary. This went beyond variation, it was a true moment of improvisation.

At an even greater level of creativity are many west African physical performance styles, where there is a very strong movement vocabulary, a strong basic pattern, but every individual can develop the physicality in their own way. This can be to such an extent that Peter Badejo claims certain dances are never the same twice, although they go by the same name – each is true to its own moment. It is therefore the purest form of improvisation. Zab Maboungou of Nyata Nyata claims that improvisation is not just central to African Dance Theatre but is the criterion for excellence in the form.

To demystify improvisation further we need look no further than the jazz musician, the classical cadenza, or the performers in a Forum Theatre piece who are constantly adapting their material to deal with the intervention of audience members onstage.

Time and time again, therefore, we see that improvisation is a constant in performance, a highly sensitive and reactive way of re-arranging known vocabulary in the needs and mood of the moment.

For us improvisation is also that rearrangement, and our vocabulary is all that we have learned, and are still learning and discovering, including what has been covered in these pages.

Let us look at how we can approach improvisation in our work and how we can understand it better.

First, for us, improvisation is a way to discover and develop elements of performance which are not pre-planned. It is to discover whilst doing and being, not whilst thinking ahead. Thus it avoids concepts being primarily intellectual and difficult to bring to life because they are born in practical experience.

Improvisation emerges through contacting our sense of spontaneity, of natural flow and of allowing things to happen. So at the end of a successful improvisation something will have emerged which was not there before, and which had not been considered before.

Improvisation has a number of basic uses for us:

IMPROVISATION AS PERFORMANCE

Improvisation can be used as a performance method. Some excellent groups (Theatre Creation of Lausanne, BTZ of Zürich and later the 'Theatre Sports' teams) have so developed their improvisation skills that they can go on stage, invite subjects from members of the audience and then unfold a performance onstage based on these suggestions.

Their discipline to follow an idea, to work with one another, accepting and developing each others' ideas, is quite wonderful. The results are exciting because they are immediate, we actually see the creativity happening before our eyes, and there is always the danger of an idea not developing.

Another often cited tradition of performance improvisation was the Italian Commedia dell'Arte, although here the actors improvised around a given skeleton-story.

In this form there would be an agreed order of scenes, with which characters should appear in each scene and what the main objective should be. It might be 'Pantalone declares his love for Isabella' or 'Harlequin steals a sausage'. The whole skeleton scenario (*canovaccio*) for a scene or play could be written on one sheet. The actors were then free to fill out this structure during the performance following their own inspiration from within their mask characters. Interestingly the actors could also insert into this structure, at an agreed signal, short set-pieces (often a fast verbal exchange or an acrobatic sequence) known as 'lazzi'.

These are instances of improvisation as the major part of a performance. In many other theatre styles greater or lesser degrees of improvisation form part of a performance, where a particular space is left for the performer to create 'in the moment'.

In recent forms of Theatre for Development these skills have become vital for a different type of interactivity. Forum Theatre and similar styles which pre-date it or which have grown out of it include a vital section of the performance in which audience members take the stage to perform. They play out what they would do to change the outcome of a piece of theatre they have just seen. The audience member is, of course, improvising, but so must the actors on stage. They must be alert to the new initiatives and actions brought by the audience member. They may have to stay in character and interact with the new initiative, or they may have to create, on the spot, new situations and characters to contain the newcomer's ideas. There is no time to plan but by knowing the subject matter of their performance they can improvise new worlds and new outcomes immediately.

Interestingly as this type of interactive theatre is used more and more throughout the world we see different styles of performance as the local medium for improvisation. In Zambia certain Nyau forms are used, in north-west India Bhavai folk theatre is used. In other words the local theatrical vocabulary, with its local resonances, becomes the currency for interactivity.

IMPROVISATION AS A REHEARSAL PROCESS

This is in far more common usage as it can be applied to a range of theatrical work. It is particularly useful if the group is devising its own production, where only the theme and a skeleton structure of the piece are known. If a performance is being devised from a given story, improvisation is often used to develop the story's theatrical life and possibilities.

Even when working with a given, well-written play, improvisation is a way of finding how the characters work, react and interact, or how a moment in a play can best be achieved, how a character's 'subtext' can be revealed, or how a level of stylisation can elevate the written words.

Improvisation is not only useful to give life to the words of a play but also to find what happens between the words.

IMPROVISATION AS A PRE-REHEARSAL PROCESS

When a new group comes together to train or to rehearse, improvisation can provide the means of learning each other's ways of working, and of how to develop a level of understanding and communication whilst playing.

Many groups play games and of course games are well structured improvisations. As these games develop into character, spatial or story-telling improvisations, it is possible to evolve ways of working together. They also make us aware of the different sensitivities we need to perform with each individual in the group. This is vital in developing that subtle, unspoken network of communication between performers which is normally seen only in long-existing ensembles.

Underlying all these 'applications' of improvisation is one basic strength: by learning to improvise, actors can gain confidence in their own ability to be creative, and to be part of the creative process of making theatre.

In doing so they free themselves from the danger of being only well-trained puppets for the director's ideas.

For our own work on improvisation we can divide the various possibilities as follows:

SOMETHING FROM NOTHING – A WORKING CONTRADICTION

This is the most basic and the most difficult. When you enter the space you know absolutely nothing of what will happen, and there are no given rules or circumstances. Working solo this is intensely difficult because we have to choose from so many possibilities. Working with a partner it is exactly what we have already done in the eye contact game which starts with no plan, no situation (see Chapter 1). As we have seen, an unending series of situations and relationships can emerge from this.

WITH CERTAIN RULES

The actor is given a set of conditions to start the improvisation, and within these he or she starts to explore and create.

This is the largest body of improvisation since the 'givens' can be re-created for each situation, and are linked to whatever type of discovery is sought. The 'givens' can be physical characteristics, a situation, objects in the room, an emotion or just new rules for a new game.

VARIATION ON GIVEN ABSOLUTES

This is really a different type of improvisation. In Kathakali and in Noh, and in some musical styles, improvisation is based on a new variation of set vocabulary. The Kathakali actor does not invent new steps, but he can vary the sequence of those which are well defined. Thus this freedom is in the order, the juxtaposition and perhaps the rhythm and strength of unalterable 'building blocks'.

Practitioners of Japanese martial arts will recognise the term 'kata', meaning a set series of movements. The same term is used in Kabuki as a movement sequence which can be adapted to different situations.

However, as we shall see, this can be a very useful type of improvisation for actors. When they are not allowed to constantly create new gestures and moves, they are obliged to discover how they can 'colour' the mood of a given set of moves, how they can fill a given shape and start to work with more subtle inner changes in the work.

PRE-PLANNED WORK (DEVISING)

This is the type of work where a group might be given half an hour to go away and work on a theme, then come back and show it. It may be called improvisation but this is really to stretch the definition, because in such an exercise very little is discovered in action. It is really a pre-decided, pre-rehearsed piece which brings together the ideas of the group's members or, when one assumes the role of director, it is the ideas and values of one person.

This is not to devalue this type of work. It often produces excellent results by giving practical life to practical ideas, but it is not creating in the moment of action.

IMPROVISATION – THE FIRST STEPS

It is vital not to pre-plan.

It is vital to be alive, alert and ready for any impulse, and ready to follow it. In initial improvisations you should even be ready to react to external impulses; a surprise knocking at the door, a roll of thunder, etc. (This is less desirable, of course, in improvisations related to situations in a play, but even then be ready for anything – someone stumbling, dropping something, they often reveal subconscious truths slipping out!)

For any improvisation work we should be in tension level 4 (see Chapter 2, the seven levels of tension), and ready to go to level 5: alert, searching and decisive.

It is often useful to jump up and down energetically 10 or 12 times before turning and entering an improvisation. It loosens you and empties you both of the nervousness and the temptation to plan what you are going to do. Suddenly you are there, energised and ready to go.

The following are stages to work through to build up a confidence with which to approach improvisational work.

Exercise 56 The line

This is an exercise to do in a group, one after the other, many times. You are doing it, observing it, and having the confidence to 'go for it'.

It is a very simple framework, and the only thing to stop you being entirely successful is if you think too much! To succeed it is vital to enter the exercise without pre-planning, without thinking what you might do. Trust yourself. There are thousands of ideas and impulses in you. They will emerge if you clear yourself of obstacles.

So, first draw a line on the floor. It should be halfway down the longest dimension of the room (a diagonal is good in smaller rooms). It can be a chalk line, but you might find a taped line easier to lay and to see. The line should be approximately one metre in length.

The group gathers at one end of the room. The first person walks towards the line (remember: no thinking or planning!). As you cross the line you enter a new space. Something changes. Keep walking but walk as if you are in that new space. For example if the new space is burning hot, or has an oily floor, or is an anti-gravitation chamber, or is a very frightening forest or urban alley, then your walk will change to be in the new space. It will have a new tension, new rhythm and new movement.

The possibilities of the new space are endless. They can be real, physical spaces, emotional spaces, spaces in which you become older, younger, the whole range of your imagination can transform the space beyond the line, better than any science fiction.

The first person has crossed the line, found a new space, walked/been in it to the end of the room. The next person approaches and carries out the same journey finding a new transformation. And the next, and the next.

This is of course very simple. But many of you, perhaps all of you, will find your mind racing to think of things to do. It will be suggesting things, censoring things, judging what is acceptable, what is 'good'. The problem with this is that you are never in the moment, you are always thinking ahead and clouding your ability to react genuinely.

At first only you will know if you are doing this, or if you are able to approach the line with a clear open mind, not knowing what will happen. After a while others will notice if you are preparing something. The difference is really quite clear.

If you succeed you will be constantly surprising yourself with what you discover. New rhythms, new moods, new body shapes, new worlds. Theatre is about creating new worlds.

I am often asked how to silence that inner voice, the judge, the censor. Often a conscious decision to enter into the exercise openly will achieve this.

If not then remind yourself of the very first exercise in this book, the empty pot, just before you walk.

Others find it very beneficial to jump energetically several times to shake out any mental activity.

One participant walked towards the line chanting 'My mind is clear, my mind is clear'.

One more way is to slightly extend the exercise:

Two lines

Mark another line further down the path.

Now you must walk to the first line, cross it, find a new 'world', and continue in this world until you reach the second line. On crossing the second line again your world changes. You will have been so busy involving yourself in the first world that there will have been no time to pre-plan the second!

At times we have created three or even four lines down the room. Each line is a new frontier into a new existence.[1]

1 As well as helping you to find your inner spontaneity and creativity quickly, this exercise can also help you spot certain other 'blocks'. If you find yourself, or observe others, falling into the same type of movement or atmosphere time and time again, then you, or they, are probably relying on an imprinted 'type' which you need to go through and discard. For example, if someone constantly becomes an old coughing person on crossing the line, even if they have not consciously planned it, they are falling into a trap of something easy and familiar. This exercise is about surprising and being surprised, not always doing the comfortable alternative.

SOLO IMPROVISATIONS

BUILDING ON THE LINE

Exercise 57 Enter the space – be in the space – follow the first impulse

Again this is such a simple concept that it becomes very difficult in practice. This is because there are a thousand impulses, and therefore possibilities, available. The mind starts to evaluate which is best, and, in doing so, blocks you from following any impulse. By working on the last exercise, 'The Line', you have begun to overcome these blocks.

As you walk into the space choose one impulse, it does not matter which it is. It might be the feeling of the space itself. No space is neutral. Each will have a different effect on you, if it is light or dark, if it is high-ceilinged or low-ceilinged, wide or narrow, if the sun streams in one end or if it is curtained.

Allow this to affect your body. Does it close it, open it, make it faster or slower, more or less tense, etc.?

Or you may take just one feature in the space – a mark on the floor or a damp patch on the ceiling. Allow it to obsess and change you.

And this is vital. Entering a space, do not just observe it and stay neutral. React to it. Feel what reaction grows in you and allow it to emerge. Once that relationship is established explore it. There is always a potential story of one person in one room. There are millions of stories.

This is a very good exercise for a whole group to work on, watching each other and seeing when the improvisation is an honest reaction or when it is 'manufactured'. (This is almost always when it has been pre-planned!) The improvisation should only last one minute, even less. Sometimes, however, when the right openness is found the story can develop and the improvisation can go on and on.

Be quite ruthless watching each other. Do not allow someone to continue if the work is not following an 'in the moment' spontaneity. However hard this is to achieve, when you see it working you will realise just how alive these moments can be.

Exercise 58 Enter a space with one large object in it

(e.g. a chair or a table)

Now the space starts to be defined. The object can be anywhere in it; in a 'strong' position (dominating the space), or a 'weak' one (not dominating).

Any move you now make is in relation to the object (let's use a chair) and the room.

Again, follow your impulses and don't pre-plan. Allow the presence of the chair to act on you. Be very sensitive to any change in your body or your rhythm, and go with it. Do not just observe the chair like a scientist. There is virtually no such thing as a neutral chair. A chair can be (or can remind you of) the chair on which your grandmother sat to tell you stories, or the chair on which your dreaded teacher sat, or your lost lover. In other words a chair can affect your state. Does it open or close you, make you more or less tense? Which part of your body leads you? How you approach it or avoid it becomes the improvisation – you bring it to life, and this is one of the great joys of improvisation.

For the first few times I suggest you do not touch the chair as getting too close can block the action. More distance helps, rather like in the eye contact game.

Later you can touch it and do anything with it except sit on it. (This pushes you to use the imagination. The easy reaction – just sitting on the chair – tends to make all the energy drain out and you are left with nothing to do.)

Finally, when the spontaneity is flowing, you can include sitting as one of many possibilities. But how do you sit? With what physical impulse and intention? With what emotion?

Exercise 59 Enter a space with two objects

(again chairs, tables, boxes, etc.)[2]

Enter the space as above. Discover the space. Discover one chair. Discover the second chair. Let your reactions flow in a tension

2 It is a good idea to change the position of the chairs before each attempt. Otherwise there is a tendency to pre-plan what to do. Better still, change their position while the actor is preparing, turned away from the space. Then as he or she turns to enter the space it is a real surprise and so a real discovery. Our goal, of course, is that we should be able to enter any space as if we are seeing it for the first time.

111

between yourself and the two chairs. Does each chair exert the same influence on you? Are they different? (One may be safe, one dangerous, one happy, one sad, etc.)

You may feel very strongly the line between the chairs as a boundary to be crossed. What happens when, if, you cross it?

Exercise 60 Enter a space in which is another space

This is most easily done with a chalk circle on the floor. Again a new circle in a new position can be drawn each time. It could also be a circle of small stones, or whatever is at hand. Most important is that there are two spaces to work with, the whole room and the small enclosed space.

On entering the space and reacting to it, find the moment of discovery of the second space. How does this smaller space pull or repel you? When (or if) you cross the boundary into the second space, what is the crossing?

In the crossing of a frontier there are a thousand possible stories. They can be real, psychological, symbolic or mythological. The crossing is an event. What is the difference in the second space? Is it a safe-zone, a danger-zone? Does it give you or rob you of energy? Does it change your mood?

For each person it will be different each time. It can be dramatic or funny. But the second space should never be the same as the first space just as your improvisation should never be the same as the last person's!

Exercise 61 Enter a space containing two smaller spaces

(again chalk circles, etc., perhaps of different shapes and sizes)

The rules are the same. By being sensitive to your own reactions and by following them through, you bring this room to life by establishing a relationship with it. You should play with this space as you would play with a partner.

Are the two smaller spaces similar or different in the effect they have on you?

With more than one space as a stimulus there is a temptation to chop and change without developing a single idea. Resist the temptation. If you find yourself drawn into one idea, one 'game', follow it and develop it. Be assured that it will lead you to the next idea, whereas if you abandon an idea to try something else, the spontaneous flow is broken. If this happens you risk constantly returning to a zero-level from which you have to rebuild, rather than building up an intensity throughout the improvisation.

Blocking an idea and not developing it is the most common problem in an improvisation. It is a barrier of self-censorship through which you must break.

If you meet a block and it seems impossible to react further, concentrate on just one aspect. Ask how your breathing changes, how your tension changes or which dynamic is prominent in your body, and then follow this element.

Extension

Build up an environment with chairs, spaces, etc. You can even place someone who stays absolutely static in the space (asleep, sitting on a chair, curled up in a space, etc.). Entering a space and finding a person there has a galvanising effect because we find it easier to imagine a reaction to a person than to an object.

In fact the body placed like this in the space reacts no more than an object. It is our limitation that allows reactions to people to be more dynamic.

IMPROVISATIONS WITH TWO PEOPLE

A great deal of the work we have already done is in fact improvisation for two people (for example: the stability game, jumping on the moment, the meetings on opening and closing, and, most important, the eye contact game).

I often find that when actors are still learning and have not obtained full confidence, they experience a block when asked to improvise with each other. The barriers of self-censorship and embarrassment can make the beginning of a two person improvisation very halting.

However, we can overcome much of this if we start from one of the games we have already tried. Confidence in playing the game removes the blocks whereas fear of the unknown reinforces them.

If the blocks continue another way of freeing the work is to start a gentle rhythm behind an improvisation. As we saw in the work on rhythm this can give a framework within which to work. Claves or a small hand-drum are best for this, not a large, over-imposing drum.

Exercise 62 The eye contact game

All we do here is to slightly formalise the game we have played before (see Chapter 1). Rather than doing it in pairs in a large group, we now take it one pair at a time.

Two people stand in the middle of the space about 3 metres from each other.

Make strong eye contact.

Wait until you feel where the first movement is, the first change in your body. Allow it to set you into motion. Both of you should keep moving, allowing any impulse to come through your bodies, whether to speed up, slow down, approach, retreat, etc. Follow an impulse to its end rather than constantly changing. Any relationship which suggests itself is more fuel for your next impulse.

Now that you have the full space to work in, use the elasticity of the eye contact to stretch the space between you. After a while you can use the stops and you can also build in breaks in the eye contact to react to the space.

This is a raw improvisational state. We can now start to refine this material:

Finding an ending

Work as described above but try to find an ending to the improvisation. This means building up the impulses and allowing them to rise to a high point on which to finish. This can be done by one or both participants leaving the space. It is also possible, but more difficult, to find a definite final position for both of you.

What is vital is that the two people must be working together to find an ending, not fighting to impose their ideas on each other.

Add a chair to the space

Start with the eye contact improvisation. When it is beginning to work well allow the presence of the chair to affect you both (but not necessarily equally). You can break eye contact with your partner to look at the chair. As in the solo improvisations the position of the chair in the room is important. In effect this becomes a game between three of you, the chair providing the third impulse.

Avoid only observing the chair, react to it.

The possible directions for this improvisation are too numerous to list here. It is important to follow the impulses and to be very sensitive to what is happening.

Do not block your partner. If an impulse emerges from your partner it is part of your game – go with it. If you do not, the flow cannot evolve and it becomes a battle of two 'egos' to impose their will.

Strangely this almost never happens in the 'original' eye contact game (when you are working, unobserved, in a larger group), only when it is perceived to be an improvisation in front of others![3]

Be careful about one other tendency, which is to put the chair between you as an obstacle. This is not wrong, but it is very limiting and leads to opposition rather than construction. The two of you discovering together the effect and force of the chair, in the room and on you, will take you much further.

And then try to find an ending to this improvisation.

Then try:

- Eye contact with two chairs
- Eye contact with a space (chalked circle)
- Eye contact with two spaces
- Eye contact with objects and spaces (a mini-environment).

By following this progression (as in the solo improvisations) you can slowly bring spaces to life and construct meanings, situations and stories in them.

Don't block. Don't pre-plan. Don't observe. Just keep reacting and follow the impulse to its extreme. That way the improvisation will flow.

3 At a later stage 'constructive blocking' may be possible. This is not refusing your partner and reducing the play to zero. Rather it is giving a strong opposite proposal to be followed. When working on certain situations this might be very useful.

If you have not already done so repeat the sequence with a rhythmic pulse as a background.

EXTENDING THE IMPROVISATION

We have not yet worked specifically with emotions and character, although these will certainly have emerged from much of the work so far.

All the improvisations outlined above can, however, be adapted to more specific searching into a desired character type or a desired moment.

If you are looking for how particular characters may interact you can begin by taking one aspect of that character to 'colour' the improvisation.

For example, one may be an open and one a closed character, discovering a space together. The physical difference will begin to establish the relationship.

You could also colour the characters with different levels of tension, or with different body parts (e.g. one with high shoulders, one with sunken chest), or with different 'element identification' (e.g. one fire character meets and discovers with one water character; see Chapter 2, Element identification). Soon a scene is developing with its own story.

IMPROVISATION WITH VARIATION OF ABSOLUTES

Exercise 63 The five movements – the kata

This is a very important improvisation exercise as it obliges the actor to discover deeper ways of reacting than the easily available cliché gestures and stereotype body language which are so often used.

The actor is required to put together a short sequence of five movements in an order which can be constantly repeated.

These should be:

1 A walk of some kind (with a set number of steps)
2 A way of dropping to the floor and rising again
3 A jump
4 A turn
5 A position in balance.

Choose five movements with which you feel comfortable and arrange them in a sequence in any order. Once set, however, you should be able to repeat your five movements in a cycle from 1 to 5, straight back to 1, and so on.

Practise this for 10 minutes to make a smooth flowing sequence. This sequence is now set. It is the 'kata' which can be applied to improvisational work.

Step 1

Everybody in the group should run through the sequences they have composed together in the space. As you go through your sequence note the presence of the other people. You cannot change your movements but with slight adjustments of speed, timing, tension and direction you can react to the others around you and to the movements they are doing. For example, you may find that your going to the ground seems 'triggered' by someone else's jump, or that two of you are in a balance together and can hold it until you both evolve into the next movement.

Step 2

Two people meet each other using only their five movements. First, keep moving through the sequences together, maintaining eye contact for as long as the movements allow. Watch for, and use, any rhythms which coincide, e.g. you may accidentally suddenly sink to the ground together, or one may rise as the other falls. Use such moments to react further perhaps by a change of pace or tension. These 'accidents' are a vital part of our creativity. They may be accidents but we have to be alert and prepared to use them.[4]

There may be movements which turn you momentarily away from your partner. Use them. Does it suggest dislike, caution, flirtation? Allow all these details to build up into a relationship expressed through the slight variations of speed, tension and direction in your movements. But the movements stay the same.

4 'Chance favours the prepared mind.' Louis Pasteur, on the apparently accidental discoveries in his laboratory.

117

Step 3

Two people use the five movements for a meeting of a specific emotion:

- a joyful meeting
- an angry meeting
- a jealous meeting
- a tender meeting
- an insulting meeting
- a flirtatious meeting
- etc.

You may still use only the given movements in your decided order. You cannot add extra gestures or change the shape of any movement. You can only play with the inner timing and tension of those movements. Yet these movements can become very flexible, very capable of different expression. Even a movement which at first seems quite out of place for a certain emotion can become part of such an expression (e.g. lying back on the floor may seem unlikely for an aggressive meeting, but it could be a feint, a false relaxation to deceive your partner; it could be a taunt). You will find yourself emphasising some movements more, others less. This is fine as long as all are completely executed.

Solos

There are many themes which you can devise for solo use of the five movements. Here are just a few:

The escape

Behind you is a prison camp from which you are escaping. In front of you is freedom. There is a tension between the care you must take not to be discovered and the yearning to be free. With your five movements, repeated as often as you like, cross the room in this situation.

The child

There is a bundle of rags in the space. You enter. It is your child. It is dead. How do you play this situation with your five movements?

The child 2

You enter having been told your child is dead. On arrival you discover it is still alive.

Since there is no question of changing the movements, nor of adding any gestures, it is as if we 'colour' the same five movements each time with a strong 'essence' of each emotion. We pour this through the movements to give a new emotional statement.

This is an extremely good exercise for those actors who tend to overact. It forces them back inside themselves to discover what are the fundamental changes in the body brought about by an emotion.

The kata of five movements can be changed to include any combinations of types of movements. Those given here are a good example and take us through different types of energies in movement, but other combinations can be created which may suit the theme of your work better.[5]

5 Actors are like houses:

   Some actors show us the great detail of the house-front, in all its technical, architectural and decorative finesse and imagination. This is very impressive.

   Other actors open the doors and windows and let us see inside the house. This is great.

A GROUP IMPROVISATION

Exercise 64 The chorus on the plateau

This is a game derived from the chorus of the ancient Greek theatre. It is based on how the chorus may have moved in relation to the protagonist on the circular stage of the amphitheatre. I have adapted it from a version taught by Jacques Lecoq, but I have met it in various forms taught by many people.

It demands a sense of spatial balance which can be adapted to any stage. It also develops a very strong awareness of a group moving as a single body, which can be intensely powerful.

Imagine your space to be a disc or plateau around which you all stand. It is balanced on a central point. If you stand at the centre this disc is in balance. If you leave the centre it starts to tilt, and someone must balance you.

Game 1

About nine people stand around the edge of the space. One person moves to the centre (it is preferable not to mark the centre point but for everyone to feel where it is). This first person feels the balance in the centre then makes a deliberate move off-centre and thus out of balance.

As the plateau starts to 'tilt' the person most conveniently placed to enter the plateau and balance it moves quickly to this position.

The newcomer is now the leader. Wherever he or she goes the first person must move to maintain the plateau's balance. This is best done with clear moves punctuated with stops to make sure the space is balanced.

This continues until the first person (the balancer) decides it is time to refuse the move of the leader. In doing this when the leader moves the balancer does not react and thus the balance is destroyed.

A new person jumps on to the plateau to re-establish balance and becomes the new leader; the other two must move to keep the balance. In time they also decide to refuse, the balance is destroyed and a newcomer enters the space to lead with three people balancing, and so on with more and more people.

The most important thing, after being able to balance the plateau, is to find the moments of refusal. These should not be signalled between the balancers. They should all try and feel the correct moment for the refusal.

This game develops the sense of maintaining the balance of a space. However, because we are assuming the weight of each person to be equal, we inevitably end up with people in a triangle, then a square, and progressing to a circle.

So:

Game 2

We now assume the weight of all those opposite the newcomer to equal that of the newcomer (the leader). Now they can all stay in one body to balance him or her.

So the game proceeds in the same way except at the moment of refusal the refused leader goes quickly to join the balancer to form the new balancing group (see Figure 4.1–4.4). It is as if he or she rolls down the tilting plateau to the balancer before a new person enters to balance and lead. This group then moves together in order to maintain balance. They refuse together and the refused leader comes to join them. In this way the balancing group grows, and becomes the chorus, facing one person – the protagonist.

This chorus now has to learn to move together and to refuse together without whispered suggestions or pulling at one another as a signal to refuse. There has to be the sensitivity to stop as one group when the moment is right.

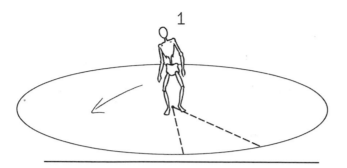

First person enters to take a balanced centre position. The arrow shows a possible first move to throw the balance.

Figure 4.1 The chorus on the plateau (1)

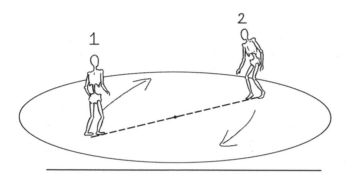

Number 2 enters to restore the balance, and becomes the leader. Number 1 reacts to every move by maintaining the balance.

Figure 4.2 The chorus on the plateau (2)

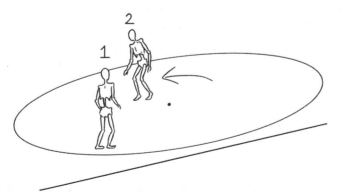

After a period of balancing when the leader (number 2) moves, number 1 refuses by not moving and throwing the plateau off balance.

Figure 4.3 The chorus on the plateau (3)

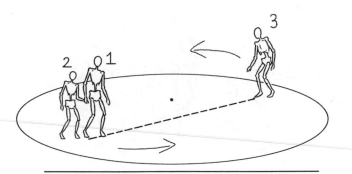

Realising the refusal number 2 joins number 1 as the first chorus group. Number 3 enters to balance their position and becomes the leader. The chorus moves to maintain the balance.

Figure 4.4 The chorus on the plateau (4)

The chorus should move as one body, not a straight line and not with anyone outside the main body. This way it can finally build up to a chorus of 15 or 16 people.

It is then for the leader (always the newcomer) to find the best way of moving the chorus around the space, challenging them, teasing, stopping or bursting into movement. However, it is not a competition to try and unbalance the space or destroy the chorus. It is also the leader's responsibility to keep them together.

As with all our improvisation work, any change of rhythm, tension, direction, body language, breathing, etc. will change the mood which will instantly be reflected in the chorus.

At this point the game ceases to be just a space exercise and is again an embryonic dramatic situation.

By adjusting the given elements you can structure this game to meet specific needs in specific plays – this is how I developed the chorus for the three Greek tragedies I directed in Bhopal. In the final performance different elements of this game were used, but the common element was that the chorus had learned to move as one body.

Extension

The same basic rules apply. The first two people play as before. Then, when the leader is refused he does not join the balancer but stays where he is. The newcomer then enters the space and joins the one who was balancing, and this group becomes the leader. When it is refused again all stay where they are, the newcomer enters and joins the previous balancers and that group becomes leader. With the newcomer always joining the group that has just refused, two equal groups build up against one another. There are two choruses, two 'gangs' in play.

5 Energy and the voice

There is a common belief that developing the voice and developing movement are two entirely different disciplines.

It is sometimes extended to the idea that those who are good at movement do not have good voices, and, on the other extreme, that if your text delivery is excellent, you do not need to move.

The most ridiculous extreme of this thinking is that the good voice and text actors are the thinkers, the intelligent actors, while those who have a wide physical range are a little less intelligent.

This is, of course, absurd. The unity of voice and body is so essential that any such division is very destructive.

Such distinctions are symptomatic of the many divisions and sub-divisions of the performing arts which have characterised European performance. In the Beijing Opera (and other Chinese 'operas') it is essential that performers can move acrobatically, talk in a disciplined heightened form, and sing. There are not separate performers for each of these disciplines. Similarly the performers in Noh, Kabuki, Yakshagana, Topeng and a host of other rich performance styles, have highly expressive movement vocabularies and equally impressive vocal techniques. Voice and body are one.

Admittedly there are some voice-articulation exercises which can be carried out with the body quite passive, but these are the fine detail. So much of the production of the voice can be made easier, can be freed, by linking it into the body movements.

The voice too is produced by control of muscles (the correct relaxation and tension from the abdomen to the vocal chords and the mouth).

The voice is a physical activity!

And there is a world of correspondence to be discovered between body and voice.

The voice can be used to create as many images and atmospheres as the body. The voice has a potential which is not only that of words; it is a producer of sound too. So I disagree strongly with those who say the voice should only be trained with and through text. It must be trained for text but not always with it.

Singing, of course, is of great use to the theatre voice, but it is a different type of projection and resonance, so we often find that good singers, with a wide range of pitch and expression, confine themselves to a narrow forced voice when speaking.

Indeed the two greatest problems when starting to evolve and place the voice are a restricted range (only working with a few notes, not using the full possibilities) and a restricted throat, which blocks clear projection and sounds harsh (and can damage the voice).

Of course all these have little use if there is not a well developed breathing delivering the air to the voice and sustaining it. We have already looked at this in great detail, but it is advisable to start all voice work with exercises to ensure the breathing is well placed.

The exercises here concentrate primarily on releasing the potential of the voice through two factors: the open throat and the full range.

We shall follow this exploration through:

- Yawning
- Panting
- Jumping
- Shoulder drops
- Abdomen pushes
- Voice massage
- Leaning in
- Voice base
- The river
- Pushing the walls
- Amplification
- Varying the voice
- Open throat calls and work songs.

YAWNING

There is nothing better. When you yawn you can feel the throat muscles opening the throat wide for the air to rush in and out. When you invoke the yawn you feel it 'take over', for it is an involuntary movement, a minor survival technique of the body to get oxygen into the system.

Yawning, and the natural stretching of the body which accompanies it, is an excellent way to prepare for voice work, and to relax the voice after working it.

If you have a problem yawning, just watch others. Yawning seems to be quite infectious. If you still have problems relax the jaw, open the mouth very wide, stretch the body and wait for the yawn to come. Whatever you do don't try to stifle the yawn or hide it behind a hand. It may be impolite to yawn in public in certain cultures, but this is the rehearsal room, and it is a must.

At first make it a voice-less yawn. Just let the air rush in and out through the open ring of the stretched throat.

Then slowly allow the air just to brush against the vocal chords to give a relaxed, low, open tone. Make sure you keep the mouth and throat open as the sound is made. If you are relaxed it will be a pleasant, gentle tone, without any harsh edges.

If there is some harshness, try to open the throat wide in the yawn, ensure that there is no tension in the neck and shoulders, and that the head is not straining upwards to try and achieve the sound.

If there is still a harsh edge to the voice, visualise your voice as travelling through the very centre of a tube and not touching the sides, even when the tube bends towards the open mouth.

After a little work with yawning this becomes an easy way to contact your open voice. But of course you cannot constantly yawn so we have to discover the same physical position of the throat without yawning.

Exercise 65 The non-yawning yawn

Stand in a relaxed position and try to replicate the muscle position of the yawn. At first this may cause you spontaneously to yawn, but after a little while you can position the throat correctly and allow the air and voice to flow through it just as in the last exercise. Again ensure that there is no harshness in the voice.

Whereas in the last exercise you had to wait for the yawn to come, you can now produce this voice under your control. Try several deep breaths and long yawn-like sound-streams, one after the other. This produces a definite feeling of the air flowing in from the space around you and flowing back out as sound which you are 'giving' to the space.

There will be a natural slight descending tone to this sound from a medium high note to a medium low note. Allow this to happen. You are starting to flex the voice on an open throat.

Exercise 66 Panting

Just like yawning, this is to enable the voice to pass through an open throat, and in particular to avoid the muscles closing the voice at the beginning and end of each breath.

Open the mouth wide and let the tongue hang loosely, even out of the mouth. Then start to pant fast like a dog which has been running.

When panting the turn-around from in-breath to out-breath is so fast that the throat has no time to close.

Having panted fast, keep exactly the same feeling in the breath and throat, and slow the panting down to slow regular breaths.

Then slowly speed it up again to the first rhythm.

When this is going well and you can feel the openness in the throat, repeat the process, and allow the breath just to touch the vocal chords on a low, neutral, breathy tone. Slow it down until each long outward breath produces this tone. Speed up and slow down several times.

Make sure the mouth stays wide open with a relaxed jaw, and that the voice is still a low neutral tone. It should be low because the vocal chords are as relaxed as possible. Avoid any higher 'tight' sounds.

It is good at this stage to have a mixture of breath and voice to allow an unforced entry to the sound. Later when the throat is free we can reduce the breathiness to transform all the breath into pure voice.

If you find that there is too much breath in your normal stage voice it is valuable to take time to observe the relationship of breath and sound vibration.

Start, always with an open throat, just allowing the breath to sound by itself. This is the non-vocalised sound we use when whispering. This is 100 per cent breath and 0 per cent voice.

Now allow the voice just to touch the vocal chords so that you have approximately 25 per cent voice and 75 per cent breath.

Increase the percentage of voice until it is 50 per cent voice, 50 per cent breath.

Keep engaging the breath with the vocal chords more and more until you pass the 75/25 mark and arrive at only voice with no breath sound.

To check yourself, place your hand a few centimetres in front of your mouth while you do the exercise. When it is pure breath you will feel the breath on your hand. When it is pure voice you should feel almost nothing on the hand. The breath has been transformed into resonating sound.

Exercise 67 Jumping

Once this basic neutral voice has been established we have to search for natural ways to release the voice from the body at a level to carry to our audiences and fill the space.

This will finally be achieved by the correct control of a strong breathing.

To discover this, and to be aware of the voice's potential, we can access many actions which naturally push the breath up through the body. At such a sudden release of air the throat opens involuntarily and, if the voice is being used, a much clearer tone emerges.

Such actions include falling, dropping and shaking exercises, but jumping is an excellent place to start.

Open the mouth wide, relax the tongue and find the neutral relaxed tone of the last two exercises. It need not be very loud. Then start a gentle jumping from both feet with the body very relaxed. As you land, the force of the landing pushes up through the body and acts on the diaphragm which 'spurts' extra breath across the vocal chords and out through the throat and mouth. It will sound like a short sharp burst of sound. Listen to it, it is a clearer voice than you otherwise have.

Keep jumping and try to feel where this voice is coming from, for you must be able, later, to reproduce this level of clarity through your own muscle control.

This jumping is a good daily exercise to loosen the voice and hear it opening.

Exercise 68 Shoulder drops

In the same way as the last exercise, begin with an open neutral tone. Then raise both shoulders as high as possible and let them drop heavily to their normal relaxed position. As the weight of the shoulders descends it pushes on the thorax, forcing air from the lungs and into the involuntary opening of the voice. Work the shoulders many times listening to that more open tone. It is your voice making that sound!

Exercise 69 Abdomen pushes

Having seen that the voice can open up with these spurts of air, we can begin to work closer to that part of the body which actually will produce that sound.

Again begin your neutral tone. Then place your hands on the abdominal muscles. These are the muscles you can feel moving when you use deep abdominal breathing. Your best position will probably be with fingers touching and the middle fingers on your navel, but this varies slightly from person to person.

During the tone give some firm pushes to the abdomen, just a quick push and release, and you will hear the same effect on the voice.

Obviously you have to be careful with this area of the body, so adapt the pushes to what is most effective, but be sure to use the whole hand to push, don't 'dig' with the fingertips.

As you get used to this there is a danger that you will pre-empt the pushes. Try to surprise yourself by varying the rhythm and frequency of the pushes. Play your abdomen like an instrument.

To totally avoid your mind pre-empting your hand-pushes, you can work with a partner. Being very careful one partner produces the voice and the other pushes their abdomen and 'plays' their voice.

As a final step try to produce exactly those same pushes, and subsequent open 'spurts' without an external stimulus, just by control of your own abdominal muscles.

These are the muscles which become more and more important in good voice production, but first there must be that relaxed neutral voice with no unnecessary tension. If the body is too tense the effects of all the preceding exercises will be limited.

Exercise 70 Voice massage

This is an extension of the jumping and shoulder exercises, since it is an external stimulus which provides a spontaneous freeing of the voice, the body producing and exploring its potential clarity and range. If there is any tension being held while producing the voice this massage will help enormously.

Work in twos.

One stands neutrally and with a deep breathing allows the same easy neutral voice to emerge throughout the exercise. Just stay relaxed with this voice and allow any changes in it to take place.

The second partner is the helper, the manipulator, who tries to find ways of working on the body to liberate the voice.

He or she follows the following process:

Start by standing at one side of your partner. Take one hand in both of yours and use it to shake the whole arm, sending ripples from the hand to the shoulder.

Then swing the arm in half-circles, then full circles. This will have first a loosening then a pumping action on the breath and voice.

Repeat on the other arm.

Now stand behind your partner. Lift your partner's shoulders then drop them several times. Then pull the shoulders back and push them forward several times. Listen for any changes in the voice, as if you are playing an instrument, and play with these changes.

Now take the head in your hands. Firmly manipulate the head down and forward then up and backward. Then move it in loose flowing movements in every direction. This is particularly important to relax the neck which, if too tense, tightens the throat. Place the head back in a neutral position. Make sure the chin is not too high, as this stretched-forward neck also tightens the voice.

With the sides of the hands gently beat the shoulders and then down the back. Then beat the sides and front of the rib cage. By changing the rhythm of your beating you change the voice rhythm too.

Very gently place the palm of the hand on your partner's abdomen and give a series of light pushes to activate the 'pumping' of the voice.

Finally bend your partner's upper body forward and down to the ground. The head should be totally loose and the knees slightly bent. Then push the relaxed back up and down, bouncing the body firmly. This is an excellent loosener both of the back and of the voice.

Slowly draw the back to a normal standing position. Check that they are standing in a relaxed, neutral way, with the head well placed and the jaw relaxed and mouth open. Allow them to continue producing the voice in this position for a few moments.

Now change places with your partner and reverse roles.

You should have felt many different qualities of voice during this exercise, many moments of opening. Knowing that this loosening is possible, you must slowly search for how to recreate these sounds yourself.

Exercise 71 Leaning into the voice

If you are still hearing some tense sounds, like a grating or rasping, in your neutral voice, it is that you are still not relaxing the muscles which surround the vocal mechanisms, particularly in shoulders and throat. The following is an excellent and effective way to allow the voice freedom.

Keep yawning, and producing the yawn-like voice. Have a partner stand behind you. The partner is there to support your weight. Slowly, and with trust, lean back and give your weight onto your partner's hands. It may just be a small angle, but you are now supported by someone else, not by your own muscles. If the partner very gently rocks you a centimetre or two back and forth, you will find the voice freed from the restrictive tensions which are blocking it.

Exercise 72 Voice base

To maintain a consistent strong tone in the voice there must be a very firm breathing. This breathing must be very deep but must also have a strong 'base' so the voice has a floor to work against.

Take a deep breath in while placing the hands on the abdomen. Feel it swell outwards. Keep the hands there and maintain some pressure on it.

Now allow a neutral tone to begin. Push firmly against the abdomen with your hands, but resist that pressure with the abdominal muscles, so that any movement inwards is slow and strong. Try to keep the abdomen in the starting position as long as possible before allowing it to push in and up. This will need a lot of resistance in the abdomen but will give a strength to the voice so it does not disappear in a quick rush of breath. In fact very little breath is needed for the voice. You should be able to produce a loud open tone without moving a candle flame in front of the mouth.

Once this strong, well-based voice is being produced, divide it in two, stopping halfway through the breath. Then start again, dividing the voice into three, then four, etc.

Be careful that you rely only on the strong stomach muscles to stop and start the voice. There should be no blocking in the throat. If there is such a block you can hear a small click at the start of the voice. Try to eliminate this by going back to the yawning and panting exercises, trusting the strength of your abdominal muscles.

Exercise 73 The River

The south Indian singer and voice-guru, Sivasankaram Pannikar, recalls his own training in voice as a young man. His guru used to take the students to a fast flowing river early in the morning. The students had to stand in the river, up to their chests, facing upstream so that the current was exercising a strong pressure on their abdomens. They then had to sing long steady notes, resisting the strong current with their abdominal muscles. Over months and years this produced enormous strength in the voice support.

The following exercise is based on that experience.

Work in pairs, facing each other, in a low centred position, knees unlocked.

One partner places a hand firmly on the abdominal wall of the other and starts to apply a moderate force, which would normally push the other person backwards. The second partner resists this to stay in the same position and takes a deep breath and starts to produce a neutral voice.

One partner is producing the force of the river flow, the other is resisting it and using this pressure to strengthen the voice. At first each breath may be quite short, but slowly it will lengthen and you will find the voice stronger from this support.

When this is achieved you can increase the pressure (a stronger 'river') and the voice base will be strengthened accordingly. In the whole of this exercise the only tension is that of the legs holding your stance, and the abdomen resisting the flow. All other muscles, especially the chest, shoulders and neck, are relaxed.

Note that again we are finding maximum performance effect by utilising a tension and counter-tension, exactly as in shaping the physical body.

Exercise 74 Pushing the walls

If you have reached the stage of achieving a strong voice through the above exercise without any tension in the voice, then you can proceed to this even more strengthening work.

Work is indeed the clue. Have you ever noticed how clear the voice can be when engaging in heavy effort? It is seen in work songs, where the voice is linked into the swing of a hammer, the sweep of a scythe and much more. Throughout the world, especially where physical labour (as opposed to mechanised labour) prevails, calls and work songs produce extraordinary sounds, and these have been incorporated into performance and rituals which reflect and celebrate patterns of life and labour.

To replicate this we must ensure that the muscles involved in the 'work' flow freely without transmitting any tension into the muscles which produce the voice.

Find a solid wall or post and find a solid low position to push at it. Start to push and increase the effort. Ensure that you are not blocking the breathing, a common mistake. By breathing deeply and fluidly you can be pushing hard while maintaining a free passage of breath. Indeed the breath helps maximise the effort as you will remember from the work on breathing.

As you push start to engage the breath with the voice until it is a full tone. The harder you push the stronger the abdominal support will be and the stronger the voice will become. If you feel any of the strain of pushing transferring to the voice, stop, yawn and start again.

This is not an exercise which can be done for a long time, especially not at first. Start with 1 minute only. Each day try it for a little longer.

The exercise can be replicated with any working action. If you have boxes or chairs to lift, or heavy objects to push try the same process; first the free breathing, then engaging the voice.

AMPLIFICATION

All the above exercises have helped to free the voice, and to avoid the tensions which can block and taint its quality. They all have the yawn as the starting point which opens the voice mechanism.

To maximise this clear sound we need to use the body as an amplifier. This has humming as the starting point. There is a great deal of vocal teaching to develop these body resonators, which I shall only summarise here, but in most cases these do not include the resonators in use in many theatre forms across the world. In particular the abdominal and pelvic resonators used in Japanese theatre can considerably expand our range and richness. These are what Yoshi Oida refers to as speaking from the anus.

The principle behind all amplification is that we can use the cavity spaces of the body to resonate and thus enlarge the sound produced by the vocal chords. It is the same principle as the body of a guitar or sitar amplifying the sound of the plucked string, or the body of the drum amplifying the struck drumskin.

Exercise 75 Hum in the head

Sit comfortably on the floor, preferably in a cross-legged position feeling the two pelvic bones against the floor, with the spine held vertical and the abdomen free for breathing. If not then on a hard chair, still feeling those bones. The beginning is the hum. To hum is to set up a closed vibration, the mouth is closed so that the sound is contained in the body. Be sure that the throat is open behind the closed lips so that the hum is easy and warm and on a note which is comfortable. The lips will start to vibrate if the voice is placed correctly.

Behind the humming lips gently bring the teeth together. Just as they touch you should feel the teeth starting to buzz. This is a sort of 'proof' that the bones of the body really do resonate with the sound. If you cannot feel this then start to slide the hum up or down your vocal range until you feel it. This glissando of pitch is vital in locating your maximum resonance, so do not stay on one note throughout the exercises.

Now gently massage the sides of the nose and the sinuses under the eyes and vary your hum until this area is vibrating. With all resonance exercises it is important to take the time to find the vibration. Varying the pitch of the hum, massaging the target area and imagining that the voice is coming out of your body at that spot are excellent ways to locate it.

Repeat this search on the forehead until it is vibrating, then into the scalp, over the back of the head, down into the jaw, until the whole of the head is resonating. Vary the pitch and see how much of a vocal range can be amplified in all parts of the head.

The chest

Now place the hand on the upper chest. This is probably the easiest resonator and it supports a wide vocal range. Keep this resonance and drop the hands to the lowest ribs on the front of the body. Massage and vary the pitch to place the voice here. Continue to the lowest ribs on the sides of the body, then round to the back of the rib cage. These can be quite difficult to locate. Take your time. These will give depth to your tones.

The above resonators are the standard ones. Make sure they are working well on a strong hum. Try to send a sound inside the body from areas which resonate the top notes through the middle notes to your lowest notes. This way you will become at ease with your own amplifiers.

Further resonators

This is a search to find vibration in the abdomen, in the pelvic bones, in the leg and foot bones and in the arms and the fingers, which you can have lightly touching the floor or the side of your chair.

Imagining the resonance travelling to these points is a good preparation; it helps the muscles relax around these points and allows them to vibrate.

Most important is to constantly slide up and down your humming range to feel when these points just start to 'buzz'. When you feel this, stay on that note and try to relax into maximising the effect.

This may take time but you will be amazed that these parts of the body can vibrate and amplify the voice.

Exercise 76 Opening the resonance

Of course the humming is only a preparatory stage. We have to maintain the resonance whilst speaking.

Start with a hum, placed in an easy resonator. Place the hand there to confirm the vibration. If you open the lips from the hum into an open sound too abruptly you will feel the vibration diminish substantially or even disappear.

To maintain the vibration, re-establish the hum, then very slowly open the lips, millimetre by millimetre, checking the resonance is still there with your hands.

As you do this time and time again on all your resonators the voice will take on a rich bell-like quality as it opens. It will feel like a stream of energy which you can direct easily to anywhere in the theatre.

VARYING THE VOICE

Exercise 77 Exploring the range

Start again with a yawn, with the voice flowing freely through it.

Allow the voice and the body to travel from high to low during the yawn. Let your body mirror this by stretching up for the beginning higher note through the arms and fingers and dropping down on bent knees as the voice slides to the lower note. Bring the hand down through the air as the note descends so it touches the floor on the lowest note – a visual representation of the tone.

Repeat this several times. Each time start with a higher note and finish with a lower one until you have a considerable range through this yawn.

Now try to repeat this without yawning, but copying the position of the voice during a yawn.

Extend the voice on one breath from high to low, back to high again, the body, stretching up and dropping to a low squat, mirroring the voice, then rising up again, reaching right up through the fingers, to return to the highest note.

Then work from high to low to high to low on one breath, and so on.

Your voice should now be running freely through its full range.[1]

Many people who have been used to Western music have considerable problems with the subtlety of this exercise. They will try to take the voice in 'steps' like the notes of a piano. Here we are looking for a microtonal variation found, for example, in Indian Carnatic music where the voice moves freely between and around notes.

1 Don't be afraid to go into 'falsetto' (high head tones) to reach your highest voice. Especially for men this may seem strange and there may be a 'voice-break' between normal voice and falsetto (the same break we hear in yodelling). Slowly you will learn to control the voice to slide through the break, by keeping the throat very open as the voice descends.

Exercise 78 Aeroplanes

This follows directly from the last exercise but develops more control. It can also use as many breaths as you need.

Play with your outstretched hand as an aeroplane. At take-off from the floor the voice is at its lowest. The hand/aeroplane can take off, fly up, level off, dive and climb all around the body. Every change of level, even the smallest, is also a change of voice pitch. The voice climbs and falls sliding rather than stepping from note to note.

Keep your eyes on the plane. Don't just keep the hand at arm's length but fly in close to the body. This engages the body fully and, with slightly bent knees, you can easily move around the room with each flight.

Clearly this exercise needs several breaths. Do not stop the plane's movement as you take a breath, just fade out the voice, breathe, fade the voice in at the level the plane has reached.

Speed and angle can both change. Play freely with the flight but make sure the voice/hand co-ordination is exact and that you reach your highest and lowest notes.

It takes a great deal of practice to achieve correct co-ordination. Have a colleague watch and check that it is correct.

When it is working well try two people 'flying' in the same room. What happens when they fly together for a moment?

Exercise 79 Image – shape – voice

This follows on from the aeroplane exercise. As if making a bold dynamic picture with a thick brush on a large canvas, make a bold shape with the hand in the air and follow its rise and fall with the voice. The voice thus makes a sound 'form' in the air.

Play with this idea. With a partner you can shape a voice picture, and your partner reacts with another voice picture. You thus form a movement-voice conversation taking the impulse from each other.

OPEN THROAT CALLS AND WORK SONGS

We are all capable of producing a loud, clear voice when we call out across a large space. People in the countryside calling from mountain-top to mountain-top, or across fields, cowherds calling in the cows, all use such a voice naturally. We also do it as children in the school playground.

It is a clear ringing tone produced with a deep breath through a wide open throat, and using the upper voice register (higher sounds travel more clearly).

Exercise 80 Call and response

Stand with slightly bent knees. Take a deep breath to the abdomen. Feel as if that breath bounces off the abdomen as if from a trampoline up through an open chest, open throat and open mouth. Produce it as a long 'Hey' sound.

Resist any tendency to stretch the chin up to release the sound. This only restricts it. In fact by relaxing the neck and bringing the chin slightly down you will greatly improve the call.

The call will be easier if you have a strong visualisation of a person to whom you are calling, and of the space across which you are calling.

When this call is ringing out, try going once round the circle, each person calling once.

Now repeat it, each person with a two-tone call. This is very common in calling. Each person can vary the tones and the rhythm of the call.

Then try 3 tones, then 4 and 5. Now there is a great deal of possible variation in tones and rhythm. Be careful you don't copy the previous caller. Every call can be different.

WORK-SONG CALLS

The calling voice can be heard all over the world where manual work is done in the open air, whether it is harvesting, rock-breaking, boat-hauling, etc. It takes many forms but one of the most common is that of call and response where one person (perhaps the work-leader) gives a new call which is answered by all the others.

Sometimes the response remains the same with the call being varied, but, in the form we shall take, the call is exactly echoed by the response.

Exercise 81

A group stands in a circle, everyone with the left foot forward. A simple movement transferring weight by stepping from left foot to right foot is set up and a working action is mimed on this rhythm. This should be fairly heavy work and the emphasis should be on the forward (left foot) step (e.g. digging, cutting, pushing, swinging a hammer or a pickaxe).

Everyone is now performing this on the same rhythm.

Over 4 beats (i.e. 4 steps: left, right, left, right) one person gives a call. This call has a wide variety of possibilities but is based on the previous exercise. It need not be 4 notes on 4 beats but can work on an off-beat, or 1 note can last 2 beats followed by 4 notes over the next 2 beats, etc.

Over the next 4 beats everybody repeats exactly what has been called, as an amplified echo.

Immediately (i.e. on the following beat) the next person in the circle becomes the caller, and again all give the response. This continues right around the circle.

Use the call as a way of encouraging the work and workers, and the response as an affirmation of 'Yes we are here, working with you'.

Avoid just vocalising the work with grunts and pushing noises and avoid sonorous 'singing'. It is a tonal call which should be able to travel large distances.

Extension of the call and response

Start with two groups facing each other. Each group is using the same working rhythm as in the previous exercise. Each group has a caller.

The caller of the first group gives a call to the opposite group and is immediately backed up by his or her chorus. The next caller answers and is in turn backed up by the chorus behind.

Slowly a relationship develops between the two groups. This is often competitive at first, but need not be aggressive; there are many other possibilities.

We are back in the world of the chorus, but now a vocalising chorus and this has brought us into a definite dramatic situation which can be developed to suit the needs of the group.

We are also in the world of theatrical story-telling. In forms across the world, from Mali to Maharashtra, the story-tellers use a chorus to keep up an echoing support to the story they tell between the responses. This is easy to establish, with the chorus having a response like 'What did they do then? Tell us, tell us now' over 4 beats and the story-teller giving 8 beats of the story in between. Depending on your story and its theme, vary the chorus response.

We have taken the voice from first opening to dramatic story-telling. It is a physical, muscular act, as strong and descriptive as any movement image. By flexing it through these exercises you are allowing it to escape a monotonous narrow range.

CONCLUSION

All the exercises, games and improvisations we have experienced have demanded your own playfulness while you are learning. In this way you can develop technical skills as well as seeing how they can be used to communicate with other actors and with your audience.

These constitute a very full preparation for you as an actor.

Appendix

Games to start the day

People come into a rehearsal or a workshop session from the busy streets, full of outside thoughts and worries, full of natural and necessary protective ways of dealing with life.

If we go straight into rehearsal or any detailed analytical work, many actors find it hard to let go of all these outside influences. They are still concerned with things from outside and cannot bring all their energies to their creative work and to their collaboration with other people around them.

This is a reason to play games to start a session. It brings people together and focuses the physical and mental concentration of the individual and the group.

The value of working as a group is tremendous and helps avoid the isolation of the individual in rehearsal which can lead to break-down in communication. For this reason I prefer games of working together, giving and taking, where each individual is indispensable to the group, and I tend not to use competitive games with winners and losers.

Of course the most important factor is that we have to *play* games, so our playfulness is instantly in action. After all, games are fun, and playfulness is intrinsic to creativity and presence on stage.

There are so many games that I cannot begin to describe them all here. Some are very good for a first rehearsal when people are still strangers – others when a group needs to generate lots of energy. Still others are good when the group needs to come to a quiet concentration. Games have become part of actor training, but of course they existed long before and it is always worth looking at the games from your childhood or from your local community.

Many of them are wonderful for co-ordination, alertness, fast reactions, rhythm and musicality.

The director, teacher or the group itself must decide which is the best for the given moment.

A great deal of skill can be learned through games but normally we do not stress what is being learned, we stress the element of playing together to have fun and to focus the energy.

However, if particular skills need to be developed for a play you might invent a game which needs the use of these skills (e.g. rhythm games), or adapt one you already know.

The following are some games which I have found most useful:

MEETING GAMES

These are excellent for when people first work together in rehearsal, for the opening session of a workshop, etc. They can be adapted to more complex use later.

Exercise 82 Name Presentation

Designed to break any self-conscious barriers of voice and body.

Stage 1

The group stands in a circle. Everyone claps a medium 4 beat rhythm, clapping the first 3 beats and leaving the fourth beat 'open'. On this fourth beat one person says their name. On the next fourth beat the person to the left gives his or her name and so on all round the circle.

On this first time around the important factor is just to project the name loud and clear on the correct beat.

On the next round not only project the voice but take a body position other than your normal neutral one. In the same way you present your name, so you make a clear statement with your body. It can be big and extrovert or retiring and introverted, but should say something about how you feel. Also make sure you place that position right on the beat.

Stage 2

The same circle, the same clapping rhythm. On 4 beats the first person comes into the circle and finds a final position on the fourth beat while speaking his or her name which can be stretched over the 4 beats:

1	2	3	4
Jo	o	o	hn
1	2	3	4
Su	ni	i	ta
1	2	3	4
Mo	ha	me	ed
			etc.

or played with:

1	2	3	4
Ravi	vi	vivi	ravi
		etc.	

Again the voice and body position are how you want to present yourself. Big or small, shouted or whispered, whatever it is, it must be clear and well presented.

On the second 4 beats you leave the circle and go back to your starting place.

On the next 4 beats the next person in the circle goes into the circle with name and body position. On the next 4 beats return to the circle. And so on all round the circle.

Stage 3

On the first 4 beats, exactly as stage 2.

On the second 4 beats, everybody in the circle copies as precisely as possible what the first person has done, all coming into the circle in the same way, saying the same name, in the same voice, as if they are acting being that person.

On the third 4 beats, everyone retires to their original positions in the circle.

On the next 4 beats, the process starts again with the next person in the circle. And so on round the circle.

THROWING GAMES

Exercise 83 Ball throw

All non-competitive ball games are very good to warm up and work together. I always put the emphasis not on throwing and catching but on giving and taking. The thrower is giving the ball and must take the responsibility of landing the ball in the hands he or she intends.

So the best way to start is that everyone moves around freely and slowly in the space. Nobody should stop so that the grouping is always changing and every throw is different.

The first person throws the ball while calling the name of the person who is to receive it.

Immediately on receiving it DO NOT WAIT, but throw it on to someone else, calling their name.

Constantly cut down on the time the ball is in the hands. It must keep travelling (this stops people trying to think or make a choice mentally and urges the spontaneous throwing to the next person).

Everyone must be very alert and looking at the ball the whole time – the ball might be coming to you at any moment. If you don't catch it the whole game grinds to a halt.

When the game is running smoothly start to move faster around the room. The ball should seem to take on a life of its own with everybody helping its non-stop course around the room.

Ball game extension

The ball is thrown as above with a name being called but we can introduce two movement dynamics; geometric and organic (see Chapter 2).

Geometric throwing is very short sharp throwing. On catching, take the ball in to the body, stop for a fraction of a second, then re-start, throwing straight to the next person; not a looping curved throw but straight and short so the typical staccato stop-start of geometric is established.

Organic throwing is when the ball is caught and the catcher takes the line of the ball and curves it round to throw again so the ball

1 The ball game can be extended in many more ways; the names can be dropped and sounds can replace them, or it can be played to a rhythmic beat to try and land the ball in the next person's hands exactly on the beat, or every second beat, or on the off-beat.

never stops. There are many ways of doing this; taking the ball and turning the whole body in a circle before releasing it, etc.

There is a tendency for this to be very slow, looping movements. In fact the organic can be very fast – it is just that there are no stops. Beware, it is much more difficult to aim an organic throw!

Change between geometric and organic and feel the difference.[1]

Exercise 84 Keep it up

This is great for group co-ordination. It is a simple concept. The group has to keep the ball in the air using only the hands and never holding onto it. Using two hands it has to be 'patted' from person to person. It sounds simple but it needs excellent co-ordination, and a strong sense of giving the ball to the next person. If the direction is not clear two people will collide when reaching for it or, worse, they will let it fall between them. Each time it is patted into the air count one more. When it drops you start counting again.

It is quite difficult on the first time to reach even 40 or 50. Reaching 100 is a major achievement. The Vidya performance group in India has reached 700!

Exercise 85 Stick throw

The stick I prefer is a fairly solid (2cm diameter) wooden stick or bamboo about 1.6m in length. Its solidity and weight make it easy to handle and throw. It also makes it quite dangerous if thrown incorrectly as it can hit and hurt. For this reason I only introduce it after the above ball games have brought everyone to a good state of alertness.

Preparation

Everybody takes one stick, and practises holding it vertically, hand in the centre of the stick, then throwing it up half a metre or a metre, and, catching it, all the time keeping it vertical. Practise throwing it from hand to hand, never leaving the vertical.

Continue throwing it vertically from hand to hand while moving through the room. Build up confidence slowly, ensuring the stick never falls!

One stick throwing

Start very slowly. Just like the ball game, call a name and throw the stick to that person, keeping it vertical. The stick is caught, thrown to another person as their name is called, and so on.

Start by throwing the stick very short distances (not more than 2 metres). If the stick is not thrown properly it will start to spin in the air and is very dangerous.

Slowly build up speed.

Then introduce geometric and organic throws as in the ball game above.

Exercise 86 The stick throwing circle

This is excellent for group co-ordination. If one person is not synchronised it throws the whole group.

Phase 1

The group stands in a circle at 'hand touching' distance from one another. Each person has a stick in the right hand. A 4 beat count is spoken by the leader. On this count the stick is transferred slowly from the right hand to the left and on the fourth beat you give the stick with your left hand to the next person on the left. At exactly the same moment you take the next stick from the person on your right.

As you cannot look in two directions at the same time, look at the stick coming to you, and you must feel where to release the other one.

When this runs smoothly, repeat the passing on a 3 beat; the sticks are given and taken on the third beat.

Then try a 2 beat.

When you get to this stage you will feel the whole group co-ordinating in one smooth rhythmic action.

Phase 2

Stay in the circle, but move back 2 or 3 paces so the circle is bigger and there is about 1 metre between the outstretched arms.

Use only one stick for the whole group.

On a 4 beat count the first person transfers the stick from right to left hand and throws it on the fourth beat to land in the next person's hand. This person transfers it right to left and throws it on the next fourth beat, and so on around the circle.

Now try again, exactly the same but only look to the right. You are looking to where you catch, and must feel where you throw. This is a little difficult at first but is soon easy to accomplish.

When the stick has been round (without falling!) a few times, one more stick can be introduced into the circle, then one more until 5 or 6 sticks are in action. As you are always looking to the right you will always know when one is coming.[2]

Phase 3

Everybody has a stick in the right hand.

Everybody is looking to the right.

On a 4 beat count everyone transfers the stick to the left hand and throws on the fourth beat (and catches the coming stick with the right hand).

So the whole circle is throwing and catching.

Then try it on a 3 beat count.

Then on a 2 beat count.

Exercise 87 The running stick circle

Everyone stands in a circle, with a stick in the left hand.

One person runs clockwise around the inside of the circle, about 1 metre from the people. He or she also has a stick in the left hand. The running must be regular and rhythmic. This rhythm should be unbroken.

The runner calls the name of someone still a little way ahead. On passing this person the runner throws the stick to be caught in the

2 As soon as you hear a stick drop, stop the action, as you may be throwing the stick to someone who is not prepared for it.

right hand. At the same time the same person throws their stick to land in the runner's path and to be caught in the right hand. Then it is immediately transferred to the left hand.

The runner calls another name, and, on passing, the same exchange of sticks takes place. And again, and again. Finally as soon as the runner catches one stick the next name should be called, so there is barely a moment when sticks are not in the air.

As it becomes easier, increase the pace of the running.

Continue for about 1 minute, then change to another runner.

This becomes a highly concentrated, highly skilled, and very exciting game.

FURTHER GAMES

Exercise 88 Ta ki wa – Ta ki ke

From a Tanzanian game taught by Juma Bakari.

Everybody stands in a tight group.

One person leads. This leader has only the words 'Ta ki wa' to vocalise and physicalise. He or she can move anywhere in the space and interpret the phrase in any way, finishing in a clear position.

When it has been said once, the rest of the group copies exactly the movement and the vocal pattern, but they use the words 'Ta ki ke'.

It can be said fast or slow, condensed or extended (e.g. Taa ki kekekekekeke), but the leader should be trying to tell a story with these word, not just play with them.

He or she should develop the story, and bring it to a close (perhaps over about 20 moves), and then tap another person on the head to take over as leader.

This way the whole group can take part in a non-stop journey around the room, exercising the imagination with a 'chorus' back-up.

This is one of many games which use one phrase, often a nonsense phrase, in many different ways to bring out emotions, stories and situations.

Exercise 89 The drop-behind circle

From a game found from Zambia to India.

Everyone sits in a circle, facing inwards, hands on the floor at your sides. You may not look behind!

One person walks around behind this circle with a ball of cloth.

This person has to place it behind someone without their noticing, and then try to make a complete circle to get back to that person's place before they have discovered it.

If the ball is discovered (hands only), that person must give chase to the first person and try to touch them before they get back to the now-empty place.

If the first person completes the circle it is the second's turn to 'patrol' with the ball.

If the first person is caught he or she continues again with the ball.

THERE ARE MANY MORE

These are just a few games. There are many which help us break into the work. Some are given earlier in the book (e.g. The Running Clap (exercise 48) and Names and Visual Co-ordination (exercise 45)).

Some are gentle, like the trust games of letting your weight fall into the arms of a partner or partners.

Others are strenuous, like the exercise of 'burst running', where the whole group runs in a circle until they feel tired (this happens very fast!) and then tries to find, with the breathing, how to break through the tiredness barrier to find new energy resources for repeated bursts of very fast spurt running, from a jogging base.

Other games are based on copying a partner, which gives great eye for detail.

Many children's games are instantly adaptable for actors; after all these games have often evolved as a way for children to learn, in play, structures of rhythm, rhyme, co-ordination, etc.

Adapt games, make up new ones, and have fun playing them.

Index